# THE POWER
# OF ARTIFICIAL
# INTELEGENCE

## UNLOCKING THE POTENTIAL OF
## ARTIFICIAL INTELEGENCE IN DAILY LIFE

### ANCHAL RANI

**AMAZON KDP**

# CONTENTS

- **Practical Knowledge:** Clear explanations of concepts like LLMs, AI agents, and vector databases, making AI approachable for readers of all expertise levels. Actionable

- **Skills:** Step-by-step guides to building AI applications for text, image, and chat-based tasks.

- **Responsible AI Use:** Insights into ethical AI implementation, including data security, bias reduction, and legal compliance.

- **Creative Inspiration:** Examples of real-world AI applications in industries like media, customer service, and education.

- **Confidence in Experimentation:** Tools and techniques to customize and fine-tune AI models for your unique ne This ebook is not just a guide—it's your companion in embracing the transformative power of AI. Enjoy the journey! Expanded

- **Appendix:** Abbreviations and Their Full Forms with Explanations This appendix offers detailed meanings and explanations for abbreviations and technical terms used in the ebook to deepen your understanding. This appendix provides clarity on terms, making it easier to navigate and understand the concepts presented throughout the ebook

# ANCHAL RANI

# INTRODUCTION

I n an age where technology shapes our everyday experiences, **Artificial Intelligence** (AI) stands out as a trans-formative force, bridging the gap between imagination and reality. Whether we realize it or not, AI is woven into the fabric of our daily lives—from the virtual assistants that help us manage our schedules to the personalized recommendations that enhance our shopping experiences. As we navigate through this rapidly evolving landscape, understanding AI becomes not just beneficial but essential.

This E-book, The Power of AI in Daily Life, is crafted with you in mind whether you are a curious newcomer eager to explore the wonders of technology or a seasoned professional looking to deepen your knowledge. Here, we will embark on an enlightening journey through the realm of Generative AI and Large Language Models (LLMs). You will discover how these sophisticated technologies can empower you, enhance your creativity, and simplify complex tasks in ways you may not have imagined.

But this book is more than just a technical guide; it is an invitation to explore the profound impact of AI on our lives. Each chapter unfolds a new layer of understanding, bringing practical insights that you can apply to your daily routines, hobbies, and even your professional endeavors. You will find tips, real-world applications, and creative ideas that inspire you to harness AI as a tool for innovation and personal growth.

In a world filled with challenges and opportunities, the key to thriving lies in our ability to adapt and embrace change. This e-book will empower you to take control of your AI journey, fostering a mindset of curiosity and experimentation. Let us explore together how AI can enrich our lives, ignite our passions, and inspire us to create a brighter, more connected future.

# PREFACE

**A**rtificial Intelligence (AI) is no longer just a futuristic concept; it's woven into the fabric of our daily lives. From the devices we use to the content we consume, AI is revolutionizing industries, reshaping business models, and enhancing human creativity. Among the many innovations AI offers, Generative AI and Large Language Models (LLMs) stand at the forefront of this transformation, offering unparalleled capabilities in generating text, images, code, and more.

This e-book is designed as a practical guide to help readers understand, harness, and apply the power of generative AI in meaningful ways. Whether you're a tech enthusiast, developer, entrepreneur, or simply curious about the capabilities of AI, this book will walk you through the essentials—from foundational concepts to advanced applications—equipping you with the tools you need to create innovative AI-powered solutions. The content has been structured to cater to a wide audience, from beginners eager to grasp the basics of prompt engineering to advanced users looking to fine-tune models for specific tasks. You will find real-world examples, use cases, and best practices throughout the chapters to ensure that every concept is actionable and relevant. My hope is that this e-book not only informs and educates but also inspires. The world of AI is vast and full of potential. Whether you're seeking to automate workflows, create personalized user experiences, or develop creative AI-driven products, this e-book will be your trusted companion in navigating the evolving landscape of AI.

Let this be your starting point, and may it spark new ideas, projects, and innovations that will shape the future.

Welcome to the world of generative AI.

Warm regards, **ANCHAL RANI**

# FOREWORD

**A**rtificial Intelligence (AI) is no longer a concept of the distant future it is here, woven into the fabric of our daily live From chatbots that assist us online to personalized recommendations that make our decisions easier, AI is revolutionizing the way we live and work. Yet, behind every seamless interaction lies a complex system of algorithms, models, and designs that make it all possible. This ebook, "Harnessing Generative AI in Daily Life", is crafted to empower readers at all levels—whether you're a curious beginner or a seasoned tech enthusiast. It serves as your comprehensive guide to understanding, building, and responsibly utilizing AI-powered applications. With a focus on practical use cases and actionable insights, this book provides a roadmap for navigating the dynamic landscape of generative AI. Through clear explanations, hands-on examples, and expert tips, you'll gain the confidence to explore the possibiliti AI offers. By the end of this journey, you will not only understand the power of generative AI but also feel inspired to create impactful solutions that make a difference. As you turn the pages, prepare to discover how to harness this incredible technology responsibly and effectively. Let this ebook be your gateway to a future shaped by AI innovation.

Warm regards,

## ANCHAL RANI

AUTHOR **&** AI ENTHUSIAST

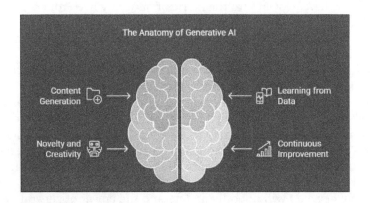

## 1.1 What is Generative AI?

Artificial Intelligence (AI) has made significant strides in recent years, particularly in areas where machines can not only understand and process information but also create it. Generative AI refers to a class of AI models that can generate new content, be it text, images, music, or even code, from existing data. Unlike traditional AI models that are designed to categorize or predict based on predefined patterns, generative AI is capable of producing outputs that are novel, creative, and human-like.

At its core, generative AI works by learning from vast amounts of data—such as books, images, code repositories, and more —and using that information to generate something new. For example, a generative AI model trained on thousands of books can write its own article or even a story. Similarly, an AI trained on art can create original images based on specific inputs or prompts.

But what sets generative AI apart is its ability to continuously improve itself. As these models receive feedback and new data, they evolve, producing better and more coherent results. This capability has opened doors to innovations that were once thought to be the domain of human creativity alone, reshaping industries and empowering individuals across the globe.

## 1.2 Capabilities of Generative AI

Generative AI's capabilities are as vast as they are diverse, impacting a wide range of industries:

- **Text Generation:** One of the most common applications of generative AI is text generation. Models like GPT-4 are designed to understand context and generate human-like text. These models can be used to write articles, create engaging social media content, draft emails, or even produce full-length books. They can respond to prompts or questions with surprisingly accurate and relevant answers, making them useful tools for a variety of tasks.

- **Image and Video Generation:** Tools like DALL·E have demonstrated AI's ability to create visually stunning images from simple text descriptions. For instance, you could ask the model to generate a picture of a futuristic city scape, and it would generate an image that matches your description. AI is also advancing in video generation, where it can create short clips or edit existing videos with minimal human intervention.

- **Music and Sound Creation:** Generative AI can compose music, blending genres or creating entirely new pieces based on user preferences. This application has sparked interest in the music industry, where AI-generated tunes are being used for background scores, games, and other creative projects.

- **Code Generation:** AI is now proficient in generating software code based on specific instructions. Whether you're building a website, automating tasks, or developing complex software, models like GPT-4 can assist in writing error-free code,reducing time spent on debugging and implementation.

- **Generative AI is not limited to creative endeavors**—it is also being applied in healthcare, education, customer service, and various other fields to automate processes, enhance productivity, and solve complex problems.

### 1.3 The Rise of Large Language Models (LLMs)

The foundation of generative AI lies in Large Language Models (LLMs). These models are designed to understand and generate natural language by analyzing massive datasets. One of the most well-known LLMs is OpenAI's GPT-4, a model that has revolutionized AI's ability to generate coherent and meaningful text.

So, how do LLMs work? In essence, these models are trained on vast amounts of textual data, which helps them recognize linguistic patterns. Once trained, they can predict the next word in a sentence or complete entire paragraphs with a high degree of fluency. This ability allows them to create everything from casual conversations to technical articles, depending on the input they receive.

The sheer size of these models is staggering. GPT-4, for instance, is built with billions of parameters (the "knowledge" a model has) and trained on diverse datasets from books, websites, forums, and more. This extensive training allows it to understand context deeply, making its responses appear human-like.

### 1.4 Transforming Industries with LLMs

Large Language Models like GPT-4 have had a profound impact on various industries, particularly in areas that require automation, content creation, and customer interaction. Here's how **LLMs are shaping modern applications:**

- **Content Creation & Marketing:**

Companies use LLMs to generate blog posts, product descriptions, email campaigns, and social media content. By automating the content generation process, businesses can focus more on strategy and audience engagement, leaving repetitive tasks to AI.

- **Customer Service:**

LLMs are at the heart of AI-powered chatbots, which can handle customer inquiries, provide information, and resolve issues in real-time. These chatbots are now sophisticated enough to handle complex queries, freeing up human customer service representatives to focus on more nuanced tasks.

- **Healthcare:**

LLMs are being used to automate medical reporting, assist in diagnosing conditions, and generate comprehensive summaries of patient data. By understanding complex medical jargon and generating accurate reports, these models help streamline processes and improve patient care.

- **Legal Services:**

Legal professionals are also tapping into the potential of LLMs to draft legal documents, perform contract analysis, and provide legal insights based on historical data. This not only reduces time but also ensures that documents adhere to legal standards.

- **Software Development:**

By generating code snippets, automating testing, and identifying bugs, LLMs are becoming indispensable tools for software engineers. Developers can input a problem or goal, and the AI can generate a solution in code, speeding up the development cycle.

- These examples demonstrate how LLMs are not just theoretical models but are actively transforming real-world applications across different sectors.

## 1.5 The Evolution of LLMs

The development of LLMs has been a gradual but groundbreaking journey. Early AI models were limited by their capacity to understand language, often producing results that were either inaccurate or disjointed. However, with each iteration, models like GPT have improved, both in terms of their linguistic capabilities and their understanding of context.

**GPT-3** was a breakthrough in AI, providing unprecedented text generation capabilities. It set the stage for more complex applications, proving that AI could produce high-quality, coherent text across various domains. Building on this, GPT-4 has refined these abilities even further, offering better accuracy, fewer errors, and more nuanced language understanding.

As AI research continues, the evolution of LLMs is far from over. Newer models are likely to push the boundaries of what AI can do, not only in generating content but also in understanding and interacting with the world around us.

## 1.6 The Role of Generative AI in Shaping the Future

Generative AI and LLMs are at the forefront of the next technological revolution. As these models become more sophisticated, their potential applications will expand, transforming industries in ways we cannot yet fully predict.

The next decade will likely see generative AI integrated into everyday tools and platforms, making tasks like content creation, software development, and even decision-making more efficient and accessible. By harnessing the power of AI, individuals and businesses alike will be able to unlock new levels of productivity and creativity.

Generative AI's role is not just to imitate human behavior but to enhance it—allowing us to focus on what truly matters: innovation, human connection, and solving the complex challenges that lie ahead.

This chapter sets the foundation for understanding the vast potential of Generative AI and LLMs, engaging readers with practical examples and highlighting the trans formative nature of these technologies.

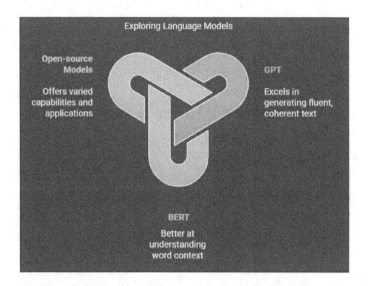

## 2.1 Understanding Large Language Models (LLMs)

Large Language Models (LLMs) have revolutionized the way machines understand and generate human language. These AI models, trained on vast amounts of data, can perform a wide array of tasks, from translating languages to generating creative content. However, not all LLMs are created equal. Different models serve different purposes and come with their own strengths and weaknesses. In this chapter, we will explore some of the most prominent LLMs—GPT, BERT, and their open-source counterparts—and compare their capabilities across various applications.

While GPT (Generative Pre- trained Transformer) excels in generating fluent, coherent text, BERT (Bidirectional Encoder Representations from Transformers) is designed to better understand the context of words in a sentence. Both models represent two different approaches to language processing—one for generating new content and the other for understanding existing text. Let's delve into these models to understand how they can be used in different scenarios.

## 2.2 GPT (Generative Pre-trained Transformer)

Overview: GPT, developed by OpenAI, is perhaps the most well-known LLM. It is a transformer-based model trained on massive datasets to generate human-like text based on prompts. GPT models, including the popular GPT-3 and GPT-4, excel in creating content that is coherent, contextually appropriate, and sometimes indistinguishable from text written by humans. Their versatility has made them indispensable tools in industries ranging from content creation to customer service.

**Strengths:**

- **Text Generation:** GPT's greatest strength lies in generating fluent and contextually relevant text. Whether you need a blog post, product description, or email draft, GPT can produce high-quality content in seconds.

   **Conversational AI:** GPT-based chatbots can engage users in natural, flowing conversations, making them perfect for customer service, virtual assistants, or entertainment applications.

- **Creativity:** GPT models are not just rule-followers; they can craft stories, generate poems, and even write code snippets based on user inputs.

**Weaknesses:**

- **Inconsistent Factual Accuracy:** While GPT excels at creating convincing narratives, it sometimes produces incorrect or misleading information, especially when the prompt involves complex or niche topics.

- **Context Limitations:**

GPT can occasionally lose track of long conversations or documents, generating text that is unrelated to the earlier context.

- **High Computational Costs:** Training and running GPT models, particularly the larger versions, require significant computational power and energy, which can be expensive.

**Use Cases:**

- **Customer Service Automation:** GPT is widely used in customer support chatbots that handle common inquiries, troubleshoot issues, and provide information in real-time.

- **Content Creation:** Many businesses use GPT models to generate blogs, social media posts, and marketing materials, saving time and resources.

- **Code Generation:** GPT can assist developers by writing code based on prompts, automating parts of the software development process.

## 2.3 BERT (Bidirectional Encoder Representations from Transformers)

**Overview: BERT**, developed by Google, is another groundbreaking LLM but with a different focus. Unlike GPT, which is primarily designed for text generation, BERT excels in understanding the meaning of words based on the context of surrounding words. This makes BERT highly effective for tasks like natural language understanding, question-answering, and text classification.

**Strengths:**

- **Contextual Understanding**: BERT is designed to read text bidirectionally, meaning it understands a word by looking at both the words before and after it. This bidirectional approach gives BERT a superior ability to grasp the nuances of a sentence.

- **Text Classification**: BERT is ideal for categorizing text, such as sorting emails into folders or labeling topics in customer feedback.

- **Question-Answering**: BERT can be fine-tuned to answer questions by understanding and extracting the relevant parts of a given text, making it useful for search engines and customer service bots.

**Weaknesses:**

- **Limited Text Generation:** BERT is not built for generating text like GPT. While it excels at understanding, its text generation capabilities are limited, often resulting in fragmented or incomplete sentences.

- **Longer Training Time:** Fine-tuning BERT for specific tasks requires more computational effort and time than GPT models.

- **Not as Versatile:** BERT's primary strength lies in understanding language, which limits its flexibility for creative tasks like text generation or storytelling.

## Use Cases:

- **Search Engine Optimization (SEO):** BERT helps search engines like Google better understand user queries and return more relevant results.

- **Sentiment Analysis:** Companies use BERT to analyze customer reviews, social media posts, or feedback to understand public opinion about their products or services.

- **Document Retrieval:** BERT can scan large volumes of documents to find the most relevant information, making it useful for legal, research, and academic purposes.

## 2.4 Open-Source LLMs: GPT-Neo, BLOOM, and T5

Open-source LLMs have gained significant traction, offering alternatives to proprietary models like GPT and BERT. These models are freely available, allowing developers and researchers to experiment, fine-tune, and deploy AI without the constraints of commercial licensing.

## GPT-Neo

**Overview:** GPT-Neo is an open-source version of GPT, developed by EleutherAI. While it follows the same architecture as GPT-3, it is smaller and designed to be more accessible for developers who may not have the resources to work with larger proprietary models.

## Strengths:

- **Accessibility:** As an open-source model, GPT-Neo is available for anyone to use and fine-tune.

- **Versatility**: GPT-Neo can generate text across various tasks, similar to GPT, though it may not perform as well on more complex prompts.

**Weaknesses**:

- **Performance**: GPT-Neo does not match the performance of GPT-3 or GPT-4 in terms of coherence, creativity, or context handling.

**Use Cases:**

- **Content Creation:** While not as powerful as GPT-4, GPT-Neo can still generate useful text for blogs, articles, and creative writing projects.

- **Open Research:** GPT-Neo is a valuable tool for AI researchers exploring new applications of LLMs without the restrictions of proprietary software.

**BLOOM**

**Overview:** *BLOOM* is a multilingual LLM developed through a large collaborative effort. Unlike GPT, which is mostly English-focused, BLOOM supports over 50 languages, making it a powerful tool for global applications.

**Strengths**:

- **Multilingual Capability:**
BLOOM's ability to generate and understand text in multiple languages sets it apart from many other LLMs.

- **Collaborative Development:** As an open-source model,

BLOOM benefits from contributions across the globe, leading to continuous improvement.

**Weaknesses**:

**Computational Resources**: BLOOM requires significant computational power for both training and inference, making it less accessible to those without high-end hardware.

**Use Cases:**

- **Translation Services**: BLOOM can be used in multilingual applications, such as translating text across different languages.
- **Cultural Analysis**: Companies can leverage BLOOM to analyze global market trends by understanding content in multiple languages.

### T5 (Text-to-Text Transfer Transformer)

**Overview: T5**, developed by Google, is another open-source LLM but with a unique "text-to-text" framework. In this framework, every NLP task (e.g., translation, summarization, question-answering) is treated as a text-generation problem. T5 is highly flexible and can be fine-tuned for a variety of tasks.

**Strengths**:

- **Task Flexibility**: T5's text-to-text framework makes it adaptable for a wide range of natural language processing tasks, from summarization to translation.

- **Fine-Tuning Efficiency:** T5 can be fine-tuned on specific tasks with less computational effort compared to other models.

**Weaknesses:**

- **Not Specialized**: While T5 is versatile, it may not outperform models like GPT for text generation or BERT for understanding tasks. It's a jack-of-all-trades but master of none.

**Use Cases:**

- **Text Summarization**: T5 is highly effective at summarizing long texts into concise versions, making it useful for news aggregation or research.

- **Natural Language Understanding (NLU)**: T5 can be applied to tasks like answering questions from a large body of text, such as FAQs or knowledge bases.

## 2.5 Comparing LLMs: Strengths and Weaknesses

- **GPT vs BERT:**

GPT shines in text generation tasks, such as content creation and conversational AI, whereas BERT excels in understanding language, particularly in tasks like sentiment analysis, question-answering, and text classification.

- **Proprietary vs Open-Source Models:**

Proprietary models like GPT-4 offer top-tier performance but are often expensive and come with licensing restrictions. Open-source models like GPT-Neo and BLOOM offer greater flexibility and accessibility but may lag behind in performance.

## 2.6 Choosing the Right Model for Your Task

When deciding which LLM to use, consider the nature of the task at hand. For creative and content-generation tasks, GPT models are your best bet. If you need a model to analyze or understand text, BERT or T5 might be more appropriate. Open-source models are ideal for developers who need cost-effective solutions or wish to fine-tune a model for a specific application without licensing constraints.

In summary, there is no one-size-fits-all when it comes to LLMs. The right choice depends on your specific needs, available resources, and desired outcomes. As these models continue to evolve, they will become even more integrated into our daily lives, driving innovation and enabling.

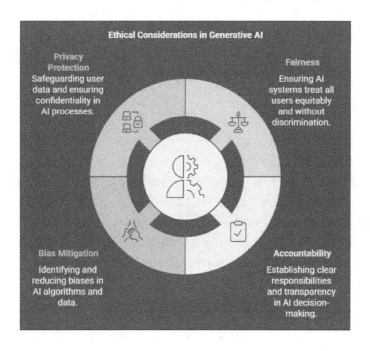

### 3.1 Introduction to Ethical AI

The rise of generative AI has brought remarkable advancements across industries, from automating content creation to building intelligent assistants. However, along with its capabilities comes the responsibility of ensuring that these technologies are used ethically and transparently. As AI systems increasingly interact with individuals and influence decisions, it is crucial to consider the ethical implications of their design and deployment.

**Generative AI** models, such as GPT and others, are powerful, but their usage raises questions about fairness, accountability, bias, and privacy. In this chapter, we will explore these concerns and discuss best practices for creating responsible AI systems that respect ethical standards. From handling bias to ensuring data privacy, building fair AI requires careful consideration at every stage of development.

## 3.2 Ethical Concerns in Generative AI

While generative AI offers a wide array of benefits, it also comes with several ethical challenges that developers, businesses, and users must acknowledge and address.

### 3.2.1 Bias in AI Models

What is Bias? Bias occurs when AI models produce results that are unfair or skewed toward certain groups based on race, gender, ethnicity, or other factors. Since generative AI models are trained on vast datasets collected from the internet, they can inadvertently learn and replicate biases present in the data. This can lead to discriminatory or harmful outputs, even when the intent was neutral.

**Types of Bias:**

- **Pre-existing Bias:** AI models inherit biases from the training data, which often contains imbalances in representation or stereotypes. For example, if a model is trained primarily on text from Western sources, it may be less accurate or culturally sensitive when generating content related to non-Western contexts.

- **Emergent Bias:** Bias can also arise from how AI models are applied in real-world contexts. Even if a model is trained on balanced data, using it in biased environments can perpetuate inequality.

- **Algorithmic Bias:** Certain algorithms may favor particular outcomes based on the design or parameters of the model. This can result in biased outputs that disproportionately affect specific demographics.

**Case Study:** An example of AI bias occurred with facial recognition technologies, where certain systems were found to be significantly less accurate in identifying people of color, particularly Black women, compared to white men. Such biases can perpetuate harmful consequences, especially in applications like law enforcement or hiring systems.

## Addressing Bias:

- **Diverse Training Data:** One of the most effective ways to reduce bias is by ensuring that the training data is diverse and representative of various groups. This means including content from multiple regions, languages, and cultures, as well as balancing gender and race representation.

- **Bias Audits:** Regular audits should be conducted to evaluate the outputs of AI models and assess whether they are producing biased results. This involves testing the model across different demographics to identify and mitigate bias.

- **Fine-tuning for Fairness:** By fine-tuning AI models on more balanced datasets or using specific techniques, developers can reduce biases in their output. Some methods involve re-weighting data or adjusting model parameters to account for underrepresented groups.

## 3.3 Data Privacy Concerns

In an era of heightened data privacy awareness, generative AI also raises significant concerns about how personal data is handled, stored, and used. AI models are trained on enormous datasets, which often contain sensitive or personal information, leading to questions about compliance with data protection laws and regulations.

### 3.3.1 Risks to Data Privacy

• **Data Exposure:**

Generative AI models can inadvertently expose sensitive information if they are trained on datasets that include personal details. This becomes particularly problematic when models memorize parts of their training data and regurgitate it in response to prompts.

• **Lack of Control:**

Once personal data is incorporated into training datasets, individuals often lose control over how their information is used. This creates a risk that their data might be used for unintended purposes, or shared with third parties without their consent.

• **Compliance with Laws:**

AI developers must ensure compliance with data protection regulations, such as the General Data Protection Regulation **(GDPR)** in Europe, which governs how personal data is collected, processed, and stored. Failure to comply can result in hefty fines and legal repercussions.

**Case Study:** In 2020, OpenAI's GPT-3 model was shown to memorize and output sensitive information from its training data, raising concerns about how responsibly large datasets were being managed. This incident highlighted the need for improved mechanisms to safeguard user privacy.

### 3.3.2 Protecting Data Privacy in AI Systems

- **Data Anonymization:**

One of the key steps to protecting privacy is anonymizing data before using it to train AI models. This means stripping away any personally identifiable information (PII) from the data, such as names, addresses, or phone numbers, to prevent models from learning sensitive details.

- **Differential Privacy:**

Differential privacy is a technique that adds "noise" to data during the training process, making it difficult to extract individual information from the model's output. This ensures that personal data is protected, even in large datasets.

- **Consent Mechanisms:**

Before collecting or using data, especially for AI training purposes, it is important to obtain explicit consent from individuals. Transparent communication about how their data will be used can help build trust and ensure legal compliance.

- **Data Minimization:**

AI developers should adopt a "data minimization" approach, meaning that only the necessary amount of data should be collected and used for AI training. This reduces the risk of exposing unnecessary sensitive information.

## 3.4 Best Practices for Responsible AI Development

To build ethical and responsible AI systems, developers must adhere to best practices that ensure fairness, transparency, and accountability. Below are some of the key practices for developing responsible generative AI applications:

### 3.4.1 Fairness in AI

- **Transparency in Model Design:**

It is crucial to document and explain how AI models are trained, what data is used, and what methodologies are applied. This transparency helps users and stakeholders understand the decision-making process of the model.

- **Fairness Metrics:**

Incorporating fairness metrics into the development process helps ensure that the AI system treats different groups equally. Metrics such as equal opportunity (ensuring similar outcomes for different groups) and disparate impact (assessing if certain groups are disproportionately affected by AI decisions) should be regularly measured.

- **Inclusive AI Teams:**

Building diverse teams of developers, data scientists, and domain experts can help mitigate bias in AI systems. A team with varied backgrounds and perspectives is more likely to identify and address ethical issues that may otherwise go unnoticed.

## 3.4.2 Accountability and Explainability

### • Explainable AI (XAI):

Explainable AI refers to the practice of designing models in a way that allows humans to understand how decisions are made. This is especially important in high-stakes applications, such as healthcare, law enforcement, or finance, where AI-driven decisions can have serious consequences.

### • Accountability:

Responsibility for the outputs of AI systems should be clearly assigned, ensuring that developers, businesses, and users are accountable for how these systems are used. This means establishing processes for auditing AI systems and addressing harmful consequences if they occur.

## 3.5 Compliance with Legal and Ethical Standards

As AI systems become more integrated into various sectors, it is essential for developers to stay informed about the evolving legal landscape surrounding AI and data usage. Compliance with both global and local laws ensures that AI systems are used responsibly and that individuals' rights are protected.

## 3.5.1 Key Legal Regulations

### • GDPR (General Data Protection Regulation):

A European regulation focused on data privacy and protection. It requires organizations to obtain explicit consent from users before collecting or using their data, and provides individuals with the right to access, correct, or delete their data.

### • CCPA (California Consumer Privacy Act):

This law grants California residents more control over the personal information that businesses collect. It allows consumers to request details about the data collected and opt-out of its sale.

- **AI Ethics Guidelines:**

Many organizations, including the European Commission, have issued AI ethics guidelines that encourage developers to create AI systems that are human-centered, transparent, and accountable.

## 3.5.2 Ensuring Compliance

- **Regular Audits:**

Conducting regular audits of AI systems is essential to ensure that they comply with privacy laws and ethical guidelines. These audits should review data usage, decision-making processes, and potential biases.

- **Ethical Review Boards:**

Establishing an ethical review board can help oversee AI projects, ensuring that ethical considerations are incorporated from the early stages of development. These boards can also provide guidance on legal compliance and best practices.

## 3.6 Conclusion

Responsible AI development is not just a technical challenge; it's a social and ethical responsibility. As generative AI continues to evolve, its influence on society will grow, making it more important than ever to ensure that these technologies are built and used in ways that are fair, transparent, and aligned with human values.

By addressing biases, protecting data privacy, and adhering to legal and ethical standards, developers can create AI systems that not only push the boundaries of innovation but also contribute to a fairer and more inclusive society.

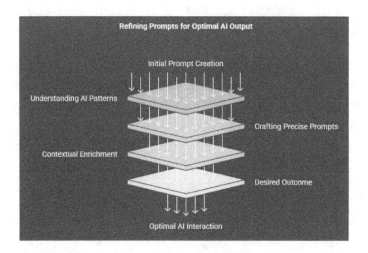

## 4.1 The Role of Prompts in AI Interaction

**Prompt engineering** is the art and science of communicating effectively with AI models, specifically generative models like GPT and others, to get the desired output. A prompt is the input text or query you provide to an AI system, and the way it's structured directly affects the quality, relevance, and accuracy of the responses generated.

With the rise of large language models (LLMs) like GPT, prompt engineering has become a crucial skill for developers, content creators, and AI enthusiasts. These models don't think the way humans do; they predict based on patterns learned from massive datasets. Therefore, the key to unlocking their potential lies in crafting precise, context-rich prompts that guide them to the desired outcome.

In this chapter, we will delve into the mechanics of prompt engineering and provide practical examples for a variety of use cases, including writing, coding, and image generation.

## 4.2 How Prompts Work in Generative AI

### 4.2.1 The Fundamentals of Prompting

At its core, a prompt is a request made to an AI model. The model then processes this input and generates a response. The simplest prompts are straightforward questions or statements like "Write a poem about the ocean," or "Explain the theory of relativity." However, prompts can also be more complex, involving multiple instructions or constraints that influence the final output.

AI models like GPT work by predicting the next word or token in a sequence based on the input prompt. The better the input, the more accurate and contextually relevant the output. For instance, a vague or incomplete prompt may result in a weak response, while a well-crafted prompt will generate more nuanced and high-quality content.

### 4.2.2 Elements of a Good Prompt
Effective prompt engineering hinges on several key elements:

• **Clarity**: The prompt should be unambiguous and clearly communicate what the user expects from the AI. Vague instructions often lead to irrelevant or off-topic responses.

• **Specificity**: The more specific the prompt, the more likely it is to yield precise results. Including relevant details or constraints guides the AI to focus on what matters.

• **Context**: Providing context in a prompt helps the AI understand the background of the task. This can involve explaining the situation, specifying a tone or style, or giving examples for comparison.

- **Directness**: Avoid unnecessary or confusing language. Simple, straightforward prompts often lead to clearer and more accurate responses.

### 4.2.3 Types of Prompts

Prompts can take many forms, depending on the task at hand. The most common types include:

- **Descriptive Prompts:** These ask the model to describe something in detail. Example: "Describe the architecture of a medieval castle."

- **Instructional Prompts:** These give the model a specific task to complete. Example: "Write a three-paragraph summary of the plot of 'Pride and Prejudice'."

- **Creative Prompts:** These encourage the AI to generate something imaginative, such as a poem, story, or piece of art. Example: "Write a short science fiction story about time travel."

- **Question-Based Prompts:** These directly ask the model to answer a question. Example: "What is the capital of Japan?"

- **Code Prompts:** These are tailored to programming, asking the model to generate, debug, or explain code. Example: "Write a Python function that calculates the Fibonacci sequence."

### 4.3 Crafting Effective Prompts: Writing, Coding, and Image Generation

### 4.3.1 Writing Prompts

When using AI to assist with writing tasks, whether it's generating a blog post, creating poetry, or summarizing articles, prompt specificity is essential. A well-crafted writing prompt includes:

- **Clear Instructions:** Specify what type of content is needed (e.g., article, essay, social media post) and include relevant details.

- **Desired Structure:** If you want the output in a particular format, state it clearly. For instance, "Write a three-paragraph essay on climate change."

- **Tone and Style:** Define the tone (formal, casual, humorous) and style (academic, journalistic, creative) you want the AI to adopt.

- *Example:*

*Weak Prompt: "Tell me about space."*

*Improved Prompt: "Write a 500-word article in a formal tone that explains the formation of black holes and their impact on the universe."*

- **Why It Works:** The improved prompt gives the AI more direction by specifying the length, tone, and topic details, which increases the likelihood of receiving a well-structured and informative response.

### 4.3.2 Coding Prompts

Generative AI models like GPT are also capable of generating code or debugging existing code. To get the best results, coding prompts must be highly specific and precise.

- **Key Considerations for Coding Prompts:**

**Clear Problem Definition:** Define the coding task or issue that needs solving. For instance, "Write a function that calculates the factorial of a number."

- **Language Specification:** Specify the programming language you want the code in (e.g., **Python, JavaScript, or C++**).

- **Desired Output:** Clearly define the expected behavior of the code, such as what inputs it should accept and what outputs it should generate.

*Example:*

*Weak Prompt: "Write a program to sort numbers."*

*Improved Prompt: "Write a Python program that accepts a list of integers and sorts them in ascending order using the merge sort algorithm."*

- **Why It Works:** The improved prompt is more specific about the programming language (**Python**), the algorithm to be used (**merge sort**), and the input type (a list of integers), which gives the AI clear instructions to follow.

### 4.3.3 Image Generation Prompts

When working with generative AI models for image creation (such as *DALL·E*), crafting prompts requires a focus on visual details. To get the best results, image generation prompts must describe the subject, scene, style, and other specifics.

**Key Considerations for Image Prompts:**

- **Subject and Scene:** Describe what you want in the image (e.g., "a mountain landscape with a river").

- **Details:** Include specific elements, like lighting, color, or perspective, to guide the model toward your vision (e.g., "bright sunset lighting with orange and pink hues").

- **Style and Medium:** Specify the artistic style or medium if necessary (e.g., "in the style of a watercolor painting").

**Example:**

*Weak Prompt: "Draw a dog."*

*Improved Prompt: "Generate an image of a Golden Retriever sitting in a grassy field, with the sun setting in the background, painted in a realistic style."*

- **Why It Works:** The improved prompt provides clear instructions about the subject (Golden Retriever), the setting (grassy field with a sunset), and the style (realistic), which guides the AI to produce a more accurate and visually appealing result.

## 4.4 Examples of Effective Prompt Engineering

Here are a few examples of prompts and the rationale behind their effectiveness across different use cases.

*Writing Example:*

*Prompt: "Write a 200-word introduction to the history of artificial intelligence, focusing on the development of neural networks."*

- **Why It Works:** This prompt specifies the length (200 words), the topic (artificial intelligence), and a particular focus (neural networks), ensuring that the generated response is both concise and relevant.

*Coding Example:*

*Prompt: "Create a JavaScript function that takes an array of numbers and returns the sum of all even numbers in the array."*

- **Why It Works:** By specifying the programming language (JavaScript), the input type (array of numbers), and the specific task (returning the sum of even numbers), the prompt clearly defines what the code should do.

*Image Generation Example:*

*Prompt: "Create an abstract painting of a city skyline at night, with vibrant neon colors and a futuristic, cyberpunk aesthetic."*

- **Why It Works:** This prompt provides detailed information about the subject (city skyline at night), artistic style (abstract, cyberpunk), and color scheme (vibrant neon), guiding the AI to generate a visually striking image.

## 4.5 Iterative Prompting and Refinement

Even the best AI models sometimes require multiple attempts to generate the perfect output. Iterative prompting is a process where you refine the prompt based on the AI's initial response. By tweaking and adding additional context, you can get closer to the desired outcome.

**Steps to Refine Prompts:**

- **Analyze the Output:** Evaluate the AI's response. If it's too vague, add more specific instructions.

- **Rephrase for Clarity:** If the AI misunderstood part of the prompt, try rephrasing it with clearer language.

- **Narrow the Focus:** If the response was too broad, narrow the scope of the task or question in the prompt.

## 4.6 Conclusion

Mastering prompt engineering is key to unlocking the full potential of generative AI. Whether you're writing, coding, or creating visual art, crafting clear, specific, and context-rich prompts is essential to guiding AI models toward high-quality outputs. Through effective prompts, users can leverage AI's capabilities to generate insightful content, solve complex problems, and create visually stunning images. With practice and refinement, prompt engineering becomes a powerful tool for interacting with AI system

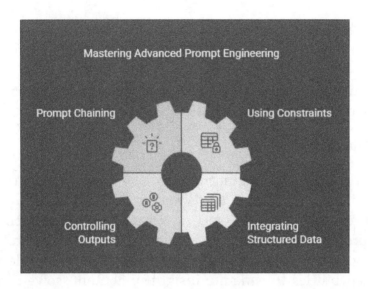

## 5.1 Introduction to Advanced Prompt Engineering

As users become more adept at interacting with AI, the need for advanced prompt engineering becomes essential for achieving refined and consistent results. Basic prompts are often enough for simple tasks, but more complex queries require advanced techniques to enhance precision and control the AI's behavior. This chapter dives into methods like prompt chaining, using constraints, controlling outputs, and integrating structured data to guide AI models.

By mastering these advanced prompt techniques, users can unlock the full potential of large language models (LLMs) like GPT, generating more accurate, creative, and reliable results across various domains, including text generation, code writing, and image generation.

## 5.2 Prompt Chaining: Breaking Down Complex Tasks

One of the limitations of a single prompt is that it can be difficult to ask an AI model to handle a complex, multi-step task all at once. Prompt chaining is a technique where a sequence of prompts is used, each building upon the previous one, to guide the model step-by-step toward the desired outcome.

### 5.2.1 What is Prompt Chaining?

Prompt chaining involves breaking a task into smaller, manageable components and feeding them to the AI one at a time. Each prompt is designed to handle a specific step of the task, with the output of one prompt serving as the input for the next. This process is particularly useful when working on multi-step problems, research-based writing, or complex code development.

### 5.2.2 Example: Writing an Essay

Consider an example where you want the AI to write an essay about the impact of climate change on biodiversity. Instead of asking for the entire essay in one prompt, prompt chaining breaks the task into distinct sections.

*Step 1:*

*Prompt: "Write a brief introduction on the relationship between climate change and biodiversity."*

*Output: The model generates a concise introduction focused on the topic.*

*Step 2:*

*Prompt: "Expand on the introduction by discussing how rising temperatures affect ecosystems."*

*Output: The AI builds on the introduction by exploring the specific effect of rising temperatures.*

*Step 3:*

*Prompt: "Conclude the essay by summarizing the long-term effects of climate change on species diversity."*

*Output: The AI completes the essay by offering a summary of the broader implications.*

*By chaining these prompts, the model focuses on each section, ensuring that the essay remains structured and coherent.*

### 5.2.3 Applications of Prompt Chaining

- **Research Summarization:** Break down research papers or articles into smaller sections and summarize each individually for better accuracy.

- **Creative Writing:** Guide AI through a multi-step story development process, focusing on plot, character development, and dialogue.

- **Code Development:** Develop complex functions step-by-step, starting with pseudocode and gradually refining the logic.

### 5.3 Controlling AI Outputs

One of the more nuanced aspects of prompt engineering is learning how to control the outputs of AI models. While large language models are powerful, they don't always deliver outputs exactly as intended unless given specific instructions. Controlling AI output involves applying constraints, setting parameters, and providing structured data that confines the response to a particular format or style.

### 5.3.1 Constraints for Better Control

Adding constraints to a prompt can limit the AI's response, ensuring it sticks to the desired scope. These constraints can include length, tone, style, or even specific vocabulary.

**Example:**

*Prompt: "Write a 100-word product description for a new smartphone that emphasizes its battery life and camera quality."*

- **Why It Works:** The length constraint (100 words) and the focus areas (battery life and camera quality) guide the model to produce a concise and relevant response.

### 5.3.2 Using Parameters to Adjust Output

In addition to natural language constraints, some AI platforms allow users to tweak parameters such as temperature, top_p, and frequency penalty to further control the AI's behavior.

- **Temperature:**

Adjusts the randomness of the output. Lower values (e.g., 0.2) make the output more deterministic, while higher values (e.g., 0.8) introduce more variation.

- **Top_p (nucleus sampling):**

Controls the probability distribution of potential outputs. A lower top_p (e.g., 0.1) focuses the output on the most likely tokens, while a higher top_p increases variability.

- **Frequency Penalty:**

Reduces the likelihood of the model repeating phrases or words too often, creating more diverse outputs.

**Example:**

*Low Temperature Prompt: "Write a formal cover letter for a job application."*

*High Temperature Prompt: "Write a playful and creative cover letter for a job application in the tech industry."*

### 5.3.3 Formatting for Structured Data Output

In some cases, users may need the AI to generate structured data, such as in tabular format or specific code syntax. Including formatting instructions within the prompt ensures that the AI outputs the response in the correct structure.

*Example:*

*Prompt: "Generate a JSON object that lists five products, including their name, price, and description."*

*Output:*

*[*
  *{"name": "Smartphone", "price": 599, "description": "A high-end phone with excellent battery life."},*
  *{"name": "Laptop", "price": 899, "description": "A powerful laptop for gaming and work."},*
   *...*
*]*

### 5.4 Leveraging Structured Data to Guide Model Behavior

Beyond controlling the AI's behavior with natural language prompts and parameters, you can further enhance the model's performance by integrating structured data or feeding context-rich inputs. Structured data allows the model to better understand the problem context, leading to more accurate and reliable outputs.

### 5.4.1 What is Structured Data?

Structured data refers to information that is organized in a clear and consistent format, such as tables, lists, or code snippets. By incorporating structured data into prompts, users can provide additional context that helps the AI generate outputs tailored to the task at hand.

### 5.4.2 Examples of Structured Data in Prompts

- *Example 1: Tabular Data for Analysis*

*Prompt: "Given the following sales data, generate a report summarizing the performance of each product in Q3."*

*Data Provided: | Product | Sales (Q3) | Growth Rate (%) | |----------|------------|------------------|| Phone A | 1000 | 15 | | Phone B | 850 | 12 | *

*Output: The AI generates an analysis of the sales data, highlighting trends and growth rates.*

- *Example 2: Predefined Choices*

*Prompt: "Pick the best option from the list below for launching a marketing campaign in Q4."*

*Options Provided:*

*1. Social media ad campaign*

*2. Influencer marketing*

*3. SEO content strategy*

*Output: The AI selects and justifies the best option based on the provided data.*

### 5.4.3 Incorporating External Data Sources

Some AI platforms allow the integration of external data sources, such as knowledge bases or APIs. By connecting the AI to structured data from external sources, users can provide real-time information or historical data, leading to more dynamic and contextualized outputs.

• *Example:*

*Prompt: "Analyze the stock performance of Apple (AAPL) over the past year and provide investment recommendations."*

*Output: The AI generates an analysis by pulling real-time stock data, offering insights based on current market trends.*

### 5.5 Experimentation and Iteration

One of the core principles of advanced prompt engineering is experimentation. Since no prompt is perfect the first time, users must adopt a process of iterative refinement. By experimenting with different structures, constraints, and types of data, you can fine-tune the model's output for optimal results.

### 5.5.1 Iterative Prompt Refinement

- *Start with a Basic Prompt: Begin with a simple, clear prompt and review the output.*

- *Analyze the Results: Identify any inaccuracies, irrelevant details, or areas where the response could be improved.*

- *Refine the Prompt: Add constraints, include more context, or restructure the question to narrow the focus.*

## 5.6 Real-World Scenarios of Advanced Prompt Engineering

To demonstrate the practical applications of advanced prompts, let's look at a few real-world use cases.

### 5.6.1 Customer Support Automation

AI models can assist in customer support by generating responses to customer queries. Using advanced prompts, businesses can ensure that the model provides accurate, empathetic, and contextually appropriate responses.

- *Example:*

*Prompt Chain:*

*1. "List common customer queries related to product returns."*

*2. "For each query, write a customer support response that explains the return process in a friendly and professional tone."*

### 5.6.2 Code Debugging

AI models can assist developers in debugging code by providing specific instructions to identify and resolve issues.

- *Example:*

*Prompt: "Here is a Python script for a web scraper that isn't working. Can you find and fix the error?"*

*Output: The AI identifies the bug and provides a corrected version of the script.*

## 5.7 Conclusion

Advanced prompt engineering empowers users to control AI models with greater precision and flexibility. By mastering techniques like prompt chaining, output control, and the use of structured data, users can unlock the full potential of generative AI for a wide range of complex tasks.

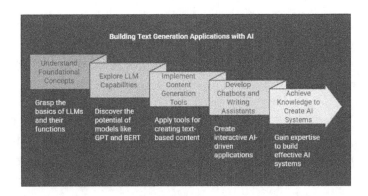

## 6.1 Introduction to Text Generation with AI

Generative AI, particularly **Large Language Models (LLMs)**, has revolutionized the way we develop text-based applications. Whether it's generating articles, summarizing documents, or building interactive writing assistants, LLMs like GPT, BERT, and their counterparts offer powerful capabilities for automating and enhancing text creation.

In this chapter, you'll explore the step-by-step process of building text generation applications, from understanding the foundational concepts to implementing tools like content generation platforms, chatbots, and writing assistants. By the end of this chapter, you'll have the knowledge to create AI-driven systems that effectively generate and manipulate text.

## 6.2 Understanding the Basics of Text Generation

Before diving into application development, it's essential to grasp how LLMs generate text. At their core, LLMs are trained on vast amounts of text data and leverage statistical models to predict and generate text based on user prompts.

### 6.2.1 How LLMs Generate Text

LLMs generate text by predicting the next word or phrase in a sequence, given a prompt. The model leverages learned patterns in language to ensure that the generated text is coherent, contextually relevant, and grammatically correct.

For instance, when asked to "Write an article about climate change," the model examines the provided prompt, identifies common word pairings and phrases based on its training data, and generates text that follows natural language patterns.

### 6.2.2 Applications of Text Generation

**Text generation is applicable in various domains:**

- **Content Generation:** Automated blog posts, social media updates, and product descriptions.

- **Summarization:** Condensing long documents into concise summaries.

- **Writing Assistance:** Providing grammar checks, sentence rephrasing, and suggestions for creative writing.

- **Conversational Agents:** Chatbots that generate responses to user queries in natural language.

Understanding these applications provides a foundation for building text generation systems that meet specific business or user needs.

### 6.3 Steps to Building a Text Generation Application

Now that we have an understanding of how text generation works, let's explore how to build a text generation application. Whether you're developing a simple writing assistant or a more advanced content generation platform, the following steps offer a clear roadmap.

### 6.3.1 Step 1: Define Your Application's Objective

The first step in building a text generation application is to define the objective of your system. What kind of text generation do you need? Is it for a specific task like creating product descriptions, or is it a more general-purpose tool like an automated blog writer?

By clarifying the purpose, you can select the appropriate LLM for your project. **For example:**

- **GPT-4 or GPT-3** for creative writing, long-form content generation, and dialogue.

- **BERT** for summarization tasks and text classification.

### 6.3.2 Step 2: Choose the Right Model

Once you've defined your objective, the next step is to choose the right LLM for the task. Not all LLMs are built the same-some excel in natural language understanding (like **BERT**), while others are designed for natural language generation (like **GPT**).

- **GPT Models:** Ideal for creative content generation, storytelling, and interactive conversations. GPT models have a generative nature, making them great for text completion and dialogue generation.

- **BERT Models:** Best for text classification and summarization. BERT focuses more on understanding and analyzing text rather than generating it from scratch.

### 6.3.3 Step 3: Collect and Prepare Data

For custom text generation applications, you may need to fine-tune an existing model or train a new model with domain-specific data. The better your data preparation, the more relevant and accurate the generated text will be.

### Data Sources for Text Generation:

- **Domain-Specific Texts:** For a specialized content generator (e.g., medical articles, legal writing), you may need to curate data specific to that field.

- **Public Datasets:** Open-source datasets such as Wikipedia, Common Crawl, and BooksCorpus provide a large volume of general text data.

Once collected, you'll need to pre-process the text to clean up any irrelevant content, remove errors, and standardize the formatting. Techniques like tokenization (splitting text into words or subwords) are essential for preparing the data for model training.

### 6.3.4 Step 4: Develop and Fine-Tune the Model

After data preparation, the next step is model development. If you're using a pre-trained model like GPT-3, you can skip this step, but for custom applications, you may need to fine-tune the model.

- **Fine-tuning a Model:**

Fine-tuning involves retraining a pre-trained model on your specific dataset. This allows the model to become more specialized in generating text that aligns with your requirements.

For instance, a GPT model trained on legal documents will generate more accurate legal descriptions than one trained on general data.

- **Tooling Options:**

- **Hugging Face Transformers:** Provides tools for fine-tuning various LLMs with minimal code.

- **OpenAI API:** Allows you to fine-tune models like GPT-3 with custom datasets using API calls.

### 6.3.5 Step 5: Implementing the User Interface

A user-friendly interface is key to the success of your text generation application. Whether you're building a writing assistant or content generator, the interface should be intuitive and interactive.

**Key Features of the User Interface:**

- **Text Input Field:** Users need a space to enter prompts or questions. The input should be flexible enough to accommodate a range of text queries.

- **Generated Text Display:** Provide a section where the generated text can be displayed. You might also allow users to edit or refine the generated content within the app.

- **Editing and Feedback Mechanism:** Users should be able to provide feedback on generated content, rate its quality, and make quick edits to improve output.

Many text generation tools, like Jasper AI and Grammarly, incorporate real-time feedback loops where users can accept, reject, or edit AI-generated suggestions.

## 6.4 Building Writing Assistants and Content Generation Tools

Two of the most popular applications of text generation are writing assistants and content generation platforms. Let's take a closer look at how to build each of these.

### 6.4.1 Writing Assistants

Writing assistants help users draft, revise, and enhance text by providing real-time suggestions, grammar corrections, and even creative writing prompts. These applications are especially useful for authors, students, and business professionals.

**Key Features:**

- **Grammar and Style Corrections:** Implement natural language processing (NLP) models to provide grammar, punctuation, and style suggestions.

- **Rewriting and Paraphrasing:** Offer features that allow users to rephrase sentences or entire paragraphs for clarity and brevity.

- **Content Suggestion:** Add AI-generated suggestions for content expansion or sentence completion.

- **Example:** Grammarly's AI-powered writing assistant provides grammar, tone, and style suggestions in real-time, helping users improve their writing.

### 6.4.2 Content Generation Tools

Content generation platforms automate the creation of written content, such as blog posts, product descriptions, and marketing copy. These tools are valuable for businesses looking to scale content production efficiently.

**Key Features:**

- **Topic Generation:** Allow users to input a broad topic and generate specific content ideas based on current trends.

- **Content Creation:** Use LLMs to generate complete articles, descriptions, or other text-based content with just a few prompts.

- **Formatting and Structure:** Add functionality for formatting content based on requirements, such as blog post outlines or product listing templates.

- **Example:** Jasper AI is a content generation platform that helps marketers and businesses generate blog posts, social media content, and product descriptions.

## 6.5 Real-World Use Cases of Text Generation

The practical applications of text generation span across industries. Here are a few examples:

### 6.5.1 Customer Support Chatbots

Many businesses use AI-driven chatbots to handle customer inquiries in real-time. These chatbots rely on LLMs to generate accurate and helpful responses to customer questions.

**Example:**

- **Prompt:** *"What are the business hours of your store?"*

- **Response:** *The AI chatbot can generate a response based* *on business information stored in its database, helping customers quickly find the information they need.*

### 6.5.2 Legal Document Generation

AI-powered applications can generate legal documents, such as contracts and agreements, based on templates and user input. These systems speed up the document drafting process and ensure accuracy.

- **Example:**

**Prompt:** *"Create a standard NDA for a technology company."*

**Response:** *The model generates an NDA tailored to the tech industry, including clauses related to intellectual property and confidentiality.*

### 6.6 Conclusion

Building text generation applications using generative AI opens up a world of possibilities for automating content creation and enhancing user interactions. By following the steps outlined in this chapter—defining your application's objective, choosing the right model, preparing data, fine-tuning, and developing a user-friendly interface—you can create powerful tools for writing assistance, content generation, and beyond. With continued innovation in AI and natural language processing, the future of text generation is bright and full of potential.

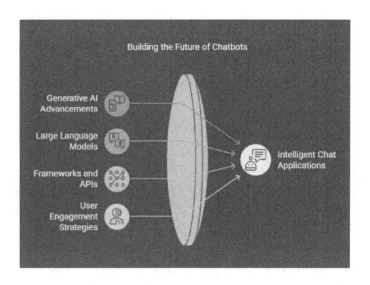

## 7.1 Introduction to Chat Applications with AI

Intelligent chat applications have become a key component in transforming customer service, user engagement, and support systems. With advancements in generative AI, particularly Large Language Models (LLMs) like GPT-4, it's now possible to create chatbots that understand and respond to user inputs in a natural, human-like way. These chatbots can handle diverse tasks, ranging from answering FAQs to offering personalized support.

In this chapter, you will learn how to build intelligent chat applications using generative AI, explore the frameworks and APIs that simplify chatbot development, and understand how to integrate these systems into your platforms. By the end, you'll have the knowledge to create engaging and efficient chat systems that can improve user experience and automate various interactions.

## 7.2 Key Concepts of AI Chat Applications

Before diving into the process of building chat applications, it's important to understand the underlying principles that make these systems work. AI chat applications rely on several key concepts:

### 7.2.1 Natural Language Processing (NLP)

NLP is a field of artificial intelligence that focuses on the interaction between computers and humans through natural language. In chat applications, NLP helps AI models understand user inputs (intent detection) and generate meaningful responses.

**Components of NLP in Chat Applications:**

• **Intent Recognition:** Understanding the user's intent behind their message, whether it's a question, request, or command.

• **Entity Extraction:** Identifying important pieces of information in the user's message, such as names, dates, or product details.

• **Context Management:** Retaining information from previous interactions to provide consistent and contextually aware responses.

### 7.2.2 Large Language Models (LLMs)

LLMs like GPT-4 are at the heart of modern AI chat applications. These models are trained on vast amounts of text data and can generate responses that are contextually relevant, fluent, and engaging. LLMs are particularly useful for:

- **Conversational AI:** Holding human-like conversations with users.

- **Multi-turn Dialogues:** Managing extended conversations by remembering context from previous interactions.

- **Task Automation:** Performing specific tasks such as answering queries, booking appointments, or providing recommendations.

### 7.2.3 Conversation Flow Design

An essential part of building an effective chat application is designing the conversation flow. This includes defining how the chatbot responds to user inputs, manages context, and transitions between topics. A well-designed flow ensures that the chatbot provides coherent and relevant responses throughout the conversation.

### 7.3 Steps to Building an AI-Powered Chat Application

Building a chat application involves several steps, from selecting the right tools to integrating the chatbot with your platform. Below is a comprehensive guide that outlines these steps.

### 7.3.1 Step 1: Define the Purpose of the Chatbot

Before starting development, it's crucial to define the chatbot's purpose. Ask yourself what specific tasks the chatbot will perform. Examples of chatbot functions include:

- **Customer Support:** Answering questions and resolving common issues.

- **E-commerce Assistance:** Helping users find products, complete purchases, or track orders.

- **Personalized Recommendations:** Offering suggestions based on user preferences or behavior.

Clearly defining the chatbot's objective helps determine the appropriate design, model, and data requirements.

### 7.3.2 Step 2: Choose the Right Framework or API

Several frameworks and APIs make it easy to develop and deploy AI-powered chatbots. Here are some of the most popular options:

### 7.3.2.1 OpenAI API (GPT-4)

*OpenAI's GPT-4 API* allows developers to build chatbots that can generate human-like responses. It is one of the most advanced options for conversational AI due to its ability to handle complex dialogues and understand nuanced language.

**Advantages:**

- Pre-trained, requiring minimal setup.
Capable of understanding context over long conversations.
Versatile for various industries and use cases.

- **Example Use Case:**

A GPT-4-powered customer service bot that helps users with product inquiries, troubleshooting, and order tracking.

### 7.3.2.2 Rasa

*Rasa* is an open-source conversational AI framework that

enables developers to build contextual chatbots. Rasa offers flexibility in designing custom conversational flows and allows for deep customization.

**Advantages:**

- Open-source and highly customizable.

- Supports multi-turn conversations and context management.

- Integration with popular messaging platforms (e.g., WhatsApp, Facebook Messenger).

- **Example Use Case:**

A Rasa-powered healthcare chatbot that schedules appointments, provides health advice, and answers patient questions.

### 7.3.2.3 Dialogflow

Google's Dialogflow is another popular option for building conversational interfaces. It integrates seamlessly with Google Cloud and supports voice-based interactions.

**Advantages:**

- Easy-to-use interface for designing conversational agents.
- Supports voice and text-based interactions.
- Robust integration with Google services.

- **Example Use Case:**

A Dialogflow-powered virtual assistant for an airline, allowing users to check flight status, book tickets, or change reservations.

### 7.3.3 Step 3: Design the Conversation Flow

The next step is to design how the chatbot will interact with users. This includes:

- **Defining User Intents:** List the types of requests or queries users might have.

- **Creating Responses:** Map out how the chatbot will respond to each intent.

- **Managing Context:** Ensure the chatbot can retain information from previous interactions for context-aware conversations.

Tools like *Rasa* and *Dialogflow* provide graphical interfaces to design conversation flows without writing extensive code, making this step easier for non-developers.

### 7.3.4 Step 4: Train the Model

For chatbots powered by LLMs like GPT-4, you may not need to train the model from scratch, as they come pre-trained. However, for more domain-specific chatbots, you can fine-tune the model using your own datasets to improve the relevance and accuracy of responses.

**Training Steps:**

- **Data Collection:** Gather conversation data relevant to your industry or application.

- **Preprocessing:** Clean and format the data for training.

- **Model Fine-Tuning:** Fine-tune the model on your dataset using APIs like OpenAI or tools like Hugging Face.

- **7.3.5 Step 5: Integrate the Chatbot into Your Platform**

Once your chatbot is designed and trained, the final step is to integrate it into your platform. This could be a website, mobile app, or messaging service. Most frameworks provide APIs for easy integration.

- **Integration Options:**

- **Web-Based Applications:** Use JavaScript libraries or APIs to embed the chatbot on your website.

- **Mobile Apps:** Use SDKs to integrate chatbots into Android or iOS applications.

- **Messaging Platforms:** Deploy your chatbot on messaging apps like WhatsApp, Telegram, or Slack using integration services.

## 7.4 Use Cases for AI Chat Applications

Chat applications powered by AI are being used across various industries to enhance customer engagement and streamline support processes. Below are some real-world use cases:

### 7.4.1 E-Commerce Chatbots

In e-commerce, chatbots are being used to assist customers with product inquiries, order placements, and after-sales support. These bots provide instant responses, improving customer satisfaction and reducing operational costs.

- **Example:**

**Bot Query:** *"I'm looking for a pair of running shoes under $100."*

**Bot Response:** The AI chatbot recommends several options based on user preferences and the store's inventory.

### 7.4.2 Healthcare Chatbots

In the healthcare sector, AI-powered chatbots can provide preliminary medical advice, schedule appointments, and answer common patient questions, reducing the workload on medical staff.

- **Example:**

**Bot Query:** *"What should I do if I have a fever and sore throat?"*

**Bot Response:** The chatbot provides medical advice and suggests booking a doctor's appointment if symptoms persist.

### 7.4.3 Customer Service Chatbots

Companies in various industries use chatbots for handling customer service tasks such as resolving complaints, processing refunds, and answering **FAQs**. These bots improve efficiency and provide 24/7 support.

- **Example:**

**Bot Query:** *"How do I return a product I purchased online?"*

**Bot Response:** The chatbot provides step-by-step instructions for initiating a return, including return policy details and shipping information.

### 7.5 Challenges and Best Practices

While AI chat applications offer numerous benefits, there are several challenges to consider. Understanding these challenges and applying best practices can help ensure the success of your chatbot.

### 7.5.1 Common Challenges

- **Understanding Complex Queries:** While LLMs can handle many types of queries, highly complex or ambiguous inputs may confuse the model.

- **Bias and Ethical Concerns:** Chatbots can inherit biases present in their training data, leading to unfair or inappropriate responses.

- **Maintaining Context:** In longer conversations, some chatbots may struggle to maintain context, leading to confusing or irrelevant responses.

### 7.5.2 Best Practices

- **Regular Fine-Tuning:** Continuously improve your chatbot by fine-tuning it with fresh data, especially as user queries evolve.

- **Testing and Iteration:** Test your chatbot extensively before deployment, and iterate based on user feedback to improve performance.

- **Clear Communication:** Always inform users when they are interacting with a bot and provide an option to escalate to human support if needed.

### 7.6 Conclusion

Building intelligent chat applications with generative AI is an exciting way to automate conversations, enhance customer experiences, and improve user engagement. By following the steps outlined in this chapter—defining your chatbot's purpose, selecting the right framework, designing conversation flows, and integrating the chatbot into your platform—you can create highly effective and scalable chat systems. With continued advancements in **LLMs** and **NLP.**

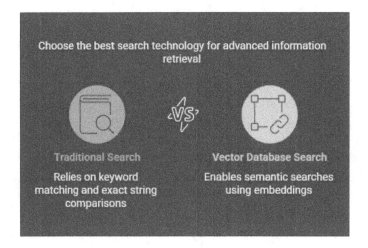

Choose the best search technology for advanced information retrieval

Traditional Search — Relies on keyword matching and exact string comparisons

Vector Database Search — Enables semantic searches using embeddings

## 8.1 Introduction to Search Applications and Vector Databases

In traditional search applications, information retrieval relies on keyword matching and exact string comparisons. While this approach works well for certain use cases, it falls short when you need to perform more advanced semantic searches—finding results that are conceptually similar rather than textually identical. This is where vector databases come in.

Vector databases are designed to work with embeddings, which are high-dimensional vector representations of data points, allowing for more nuanced and context-aware searches. Combined with AI models like GPT, search apps powered by vector databases enable users to search not just for exact terms, but for ideas, concepts, and similar meanings.

In this chapter, we will explore the basics of vector databases, understand how embeddings work, and guide you through building search applications using advanced tools like Faiss and

Pinecone. These tools allow you to create applications that can retrieve the most relevant content, even when the query doesn't exactly match the stored information.

## 8.2 What Are Vector Databases?

Vector databases are specialized databases designed to store and manage embeddings—high-dimensional vector representations of data such as text, images, or any other form of content. Unlike traditional databases that rely on exact matches, vector databases are capable of comparing the "closeness" or similarity between different data points based on their vector representation.

### 8.2.1 How Vector Databases Differ from Traditional Databases

- **Keyword-based vs. Semantic Search:** Traditional databases rely on exact keyword matching, whereas vector databases allow for semantic searches, enabling a deeper understanding of the context and meaning of a query.

- **High-Dimensional Data:** Vector databases can store and process high-dimensional embeddings, typically generated by machine learning models. These embeddings represent the core semantic information of text or other data types.

- **Efficient Search:** By using techniques like Approximate Nearest Neighbors (ANN), vector databases can efficiently retrieve results even from large datasets, providing fast and accurate results based on vector similarity.

### 8.2.2 Common Use Cases for Vector Databases

- **Recommendation Systems:** Suggesting similar products or services based on user preferences or past behavior.
- **Document Retrieval:** Searching for documents, articles,

or research papers that are semantically related to a user's query.

- **Image Search:** Finding visually similar images based on embeddings extracted from the images themselves.

## 8.3 Understanding Embeddings

Embeddings are the foundation of vector search. They transform data (text, images, or other forms) into dense vector representations, where semantically similar data points have similar vectors.

### 8.3.1 What Are Embeddings?

Embeddings are numerical representations of data in a continuous vector space. These vectors capture the semantic relationships between data points, meaning similar data points are positioned closely together in the vector space, while dissimilar points are far apart.

- **For example:**

The words "cat" and "dog" will have vector representations that are closer to each other because they share similar semantic properties (both are animals, pets, etc.).

- The word "cat" and the word "car" will have vector representations that are further apart, as they refer to completely different concepts.

### 8.3.2 How Embeddings Are Generated

- **Text Embeddings:** In the context of text, embeddings are often generated using models like GPT, BERT, or other language models. These models take a piece of text and convert it into a high-dimensional vector.

- **Image Embeddings:** For images, embeddings can be generated using convolutional neural networks (CNNs) that extract key features and represent the image in a vector format.

### 8.3.3 Key Properties of Embeddings

- **High-Dimensional:** Typically, embeddings are in hundreds or thousands of dimensions.

- **Dense Representation:** Unlike sparse one-hot encodings, embeddings are dense and continuous, allowing for more compact and meaningful representations.

- **Similarity Measurement:** Vectors that are close in the embedding space (using metrics like cosine similarity or Euclidean distance) represent semantically similar content.

## 8.4 Creating Search Applications with Vector Databases

Now that we understand vector databases and embeddings, let's dive into the steps required to build a search application.

### 8.4.1 Step 1: Generate Embeddings for Your Data

The first step in building a vector-based search app is to generate embeddings for your dataset. This involves using a pre-trained model, such as GPT or BERT, to create vector representations for your data.

**For example, if you are building a document search app:**

- **Text Embedding:** Pass each document (or section of the document) through the model to obtain its embedding.

- **Store the Embeddings:** Once the embeddings are generated, store them in the vector database for efficient retrieval later.

*from transformers import GPT2Tokenizer, GPT2Model*

*tokenizer = GPT2Tokenizer.from_pretrained("gpt2")*
*model = GPT2Model.from_pretrained("gpt2")*

*# Generate embeddings for a text document*

*inputs = tokenizer("Sample document text", return_tensors="pt")*

*outputs = model(**inputs)*

*embedding = outputs.last_hidden_state.mean(dim=1)  # A simple way to get a single vector for the document*

*8.4.2 Step 2: Store Embeddings in a Vector Database*

Once you've generated the embeddings, the next step is to store them in a vector database. Tools like Faiss and Pinecone are popular choices for managing and searching through these embeddings.

**8.4.2.1 Faiss**

*Faiss is a library developed by Facebook AI that enables efficient similarity search and clustering of dense vectors. It is highly*

*scalable and optimized for large-scale datasets.*
*To set up Faiss:*

*1. Install Faiss:*

*pip install faiss-cpu*

*2. Indexing the Embeddings: You can index your embeddings to enable efficient similarity searches.*

*import faiss*

*index = faiss.IndexFlatL2(embedding_size) # Using L2 (Euclidean) distance metric*

*index.add(embedding_data) # Add your embeddings to the index*

## 8.4.2.2 Pinecone

Pinecone is a managed vector database service that simplifies the process of storing, indexing, and querying embeddings. It allows you to focus on building the application without worrying about infrastructure.

**To use Pinecone:**

**1. Sign up for Pinecone at their official site and get an API key.**

**2. Install Pinecone Client:**

**pip install pinecone-client**

**3. Create and Upload Vectors: After initializing the Pinecone environment, you can create a vector index and upload embeddings for your search app.**

### 8.4.3 Step 3: Query the Vector Database

Once the embeddings are stored, the next step is to query

the database. When a user submits a query, you generate an embedding for the query using the same model used for your dataset. Then, you search the vector database to find the most similar embeddings.

- **For example:**

The user queries, ***"How to bake a cake?"***

You pass this query through your language model to obtain its embedding.

You search the vector database using cosine similarity or Euclidean distance to find the most relevant documents (or images) in your dataset.

- **Example Search with Faiss:**

*D, I = index.search(query_embedding, k=5) # Find the top 5 closest embeddings*

**Example Search with Pinecone:**
*query_response = pinecone_index.query(query_embedding, top_k=5)*

The results returned will include the closest matches to the query, ranked by similarity score.

## 8.5 Advanced Features and Use Cases

### 8.5.1 Combining Vector Search with Traditional Keyword Search

In some applications, a hybrid approach works best. By combining vector search with traditional keyword-based search, you can optimize for both precision (exact matches) and recall (semantically similar results). This is especially useful in document retrieval systems where both keywords and concepts are important.

### 8.5.2 Real-Time Recommendations

Vector databases enable real-time recommendation engines. By generating embeddings for user interactions (like clicks or searches), you can instantly suggest products, services, or content that are similar to what the user has previously shown interest in.

### 8.5.3 Personalization

With vector databases, personalization becomes more accurate. By storing embeddings of user profiles and preferences, you can tailor the search results or recommendations to individual users based on their unique vector representation.

### 8.6 Conclusion

Vector databases have revolutionized the way we approach search by enabling more intuitive and context-aware systems. With tools like Faiss and Pinecone, it's now easier than ever to build search applications that go beyond keyword matching and instead focus on understanding the meaning behind user queries. By leveraging embeddings generated by models like GPT or BERT, your search applications can become smarter, faster, and more accurate, providing users with an enhanced experience. Whether you're building document retrieval systems, recommendation engines, or personalized content platforms, vector databases offer powerful capabilities that traditional search engines cannot matc

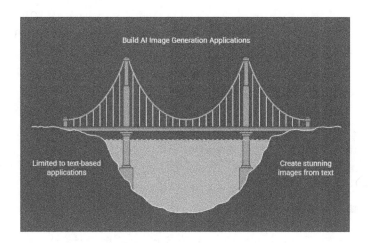

## 9.1 Introduction to AI Image Generation

The realm of artificial intelligence has expanded beyond text-based applications and now ventures into the fascinating world of image generation. Powered by advanced models like DALL·E, Stable Diffusion, and other generative adversarial networks (GANs), AI is capable of creating stunning and highly detailed images from simple text prompts. This leap in technology has opened doors for a wide array of applications, from art and media to advertising, design, and even personalized content creation.

This chapter will guide you through building your own image generation applications, leveraging the power of these models to turn text descriptions into images. You will learn about the core tools and frameworks, how these systems work, and practical use cases where AI-generated images are transforming industries. By the end of the chapter, you will have the foundation to create AI-driven applications that cater to artistic, commercial, and social needs.

## 9.2 The Technology Behind Image Generation

At the core of AI image generation lies the ability to understand and interpret text and convert it into visual elements. This is achieved using large models trained on massive datasets of images and their corresponding descriptions. Two of the most prominent models in this space are:

- *DALL·E:* Developed by *OpenAI, DALL·E* uses transformer-based architecture to generate highly detailed and creative images from textual descriptions. The model was trained on extensive datasets and can create original visuals in various styles.

- **Stable Diffusion:** Stable Diffusion is a diffusion-based model that produces images by learning how to "denoise" a series of random pixels into a coherent image. It's open-source, highly flexible, and capable of producing high-quality images from complex prompts.

### 9.2.1 How It Works: From Text to Image

- **Text Encoding:** The text prompt is first processed by the model's encoder, converting it into a series of meaningful representations (vectors) that capture the semantics and details of the text.

- **Latent Space Mapping:** In models like Stable Diffusion, this text encoding guides the generation process in a "latent space," a mathematical representation where patterns and structures of the final image are gradually revealed.

- **Image Generation:** The model uses a process of refinement (such as diffusion) to gradually build the final image, ensuring that it matches the semantics of the text as closely as possible.

## 9.3 Building Image Generation Applications

Building a fully functional AI image generation app requires several components:

A pre-trained generative model (such as DALL·E or Stable Diffusion).

A user interface to accept text prompts.

Backend processing to generate the images.

Optional features such as image post-processing, styling, and the ability to download or share images.
Let's walk through a step-by-step guide to building a basic image generation application.

### 9.3.1 Step 1: Setting Up the Model

To begin, you'll need access to a pre-trained model. Stable Diffusion offers more flexibility due to its open-source nature, while DALL·E requires API access from OpenAI. Let's focus on using Stable Diffusion for this example.

- **Install the necessary libraries:** To work with Stable Diffusion, you can use the Hugging Face Diffusers library, which provides an easy-to-use interface for loading the model and generating images.

**pip install diffusers transformers torch**

- **Load the Model:**

*from diffusers import StableDiffusionPipeline*

*import torch*

*# Load the model*
*model = StableDiffusionPipeline.from_pretrained("CompVis/ stable-diffusion-v1-4")*

*model = model.to("cuda") # Use GPU for faster generation*

### 9.3.2 Step 2: Accepting Text Prompts

Next, create a simple user interface that allows users to input their text descriptions. If you're building a web-based application, frameworks like Flask or Django can be used for the frontend.

*from flask import Flask, render_template, request*

*app = Flask(__name__)*
*@app.route('/')*
*def index():*

   *return render_template('index.html')*
*@app.route('/generate', methods=['POST'])*
*def generate_image():*

   *prompt = request.form['prompt']*

   *generated_image = model(prompt).images[0] # Generate image based on the text prompt*

   *generated_image.save('output_image.png')     # Save the generated image*
   *return 'Image Generated!'*

*In this basic example, users can submit a text prompt, and the backend will pass that to the model to generate an image.*

### 9.3.3 Step 3: Generating the Image

*The heavy lifting happens here, where the model takes in the text prompt, generates the image, and returns the result.*

```
def generate_image_from_text(prompt):

    # Generate the image
    image = model(prompt).images[0]

    image.show()  # Display the image or save it as required
    return image
```

You can further enhance the application by adding features like multiple image outputs, allowing users to choose different styles, or letting them adjust parameters like the number of iterations or image resolution.

## 9.4 Practical Use Cases for AI Image Generation

AI-generated images have far-reaching applications across multiple domains, providing creative and commercial value in ways previously unachievable.

### 9.4.1 Artistic Uses

One of the most obvious uses of AI-generated images is in art creation. AI artists can use these tools to generate entirely new pieces of art from just a few descriptive words, offering infinite creative possibilities. AI can replicate different art styles, from classical paintings to modern, abstract art, allowing non-artists to produce high-quality visuals.

Artists are also using these tools to create new forms of

digital art, combining traditional techniques with AI-generated elements.

### 9.4.2 Media and Advertising

In media and advertising, AI-generated images offer a way to quickly and cost-effectively produce unique visuals tailored to specific campaigns. Companies can create highly customized marketing materials without the need for an extensive design team.

**Examples:**

- **Social Media Content:** Marketers can quickly generate unique images for posts, tailored to different audiences.

- **Advertisements:** AI-generated images can provide personalized visuals for different regions, demographics, or consumer preferences.

- **Branding:** Logos and branding materials can be generated with varying styles and aesthetics to match a brand's identity.

### 9.4.3 Design and Prototyping

Designers are using AI tools for rapid prototyping, helping to visualize concepts in a short amount of time. Whether it's a new product, logo, or architectural design, AI tools can help bring ideas to life with minimal manual effort.

### 9.4.4 Personalization

With AI, users can generate personalized content for various purposes, from birthday cards to custom home décor. This level of personalization enhances user engagement and satisfaction, especially in industries like e-commerce and entertainment.

## 9.5 Advanced Features in Image Generation Applications

### 9.5.1 Style Transfer

One popular feature in image generation apps is style transfer, where a user can request that the generated image reflect a specific artistic style. For example, an image could be generated in the style of Van Gogh's "Starry Night" or Picasso's "Cubism." Style transfer allows users to have more control over the creative output.

### 9.5.2 Post-Processing

After the image is generated, additional post-processing features can be added, such as enhancing image quality, adjusting colors, or applying filters. Post-processing allows users to fine-tune their images for specific use cases, such as print media or digital display.

### 9.5.3 Multiple Outputs and Customization

Another powerful feature is giving users the ability to generate multiple images for a single text prompt, allowing them to choose from different variations. This enhances the creativity of the process and ensures that users get exactly what they are looking for.

### 9.6 Conclusion

The use of AI-generated images is revolutionizing fields ranging from art and design to media and advertising. With the right tools and frameworks, building your own image generation application has become more accessible than ever before. Models like Stable Diffusion and **DALL·E** allow developers and creators to translate simple text prompts into visually stunning images, unleashing creativity and automation in unprecedented ways. Whether you aim to build an artistic application or a commercial solution, understanding the fundamentals of AI image generation and applying them to real-world scenarios can lead to powerful and engaging applications that captivate users and transform industries.

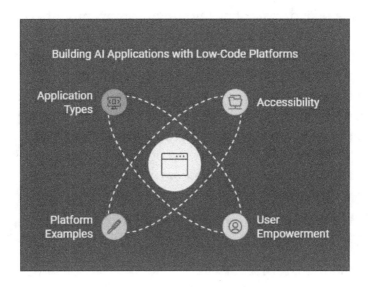

## 10.1 Introduction to Low-Code AI Development

The advent of low-code and no-code development platforms has democratized access to artificial intelligence, making it possible for non-developers and business users to build AI-powered applications. These platforms allow people with minimal programming experience to create powerful tools that can leverage AI models, such as those from **OpenAI**, without writing complex code. By simplifying the development process, these solutions open the door for a broader range of users to build custom applications for their specific needs, such as chatbots, recommendation systems, image generation tools, and more.

In this chapter, we will explore the world of low-code AI platforms, examining how they work, what tools are available, and how you can start building AI applications today. By the end of this chapter, you will have a clear understanding of how to leverage these platforms to build functional, AI-powered apps, even if you're not a coding expert.

## 10.2 What Are Low-Code Platforms?

Low-code platforms are development environments that allow users to build applications using visual interfaces and drag-and-drop components instead of writing extensive lines of code. These platforms come with pre-built templates, modules, and integrations that simplify the application-building process. The goal of low-code platforms is to reduce the complexity of app development while still offering robust functionality.

In the context of AI, low-code platforms come with built-in integrations for machine learning (ML) models, natural language processing (NLP), and other AI services, which users can connect to their apps with minimal effort. This enables individuals or businesses to create AI-enhanced tools, **such as:**

Chatbots for customer service.

Recommendation engines for personalized content delivery.
Sentiment analysis tools for understanding user feedback.

## 10.3 Popular Low-Code AI Platforms

Several platforms make it easy to build AI applications without needing deep technical knowledge. Below are some of the most popular ones that offer accessible, powerful, and scalable solutions:

### 10.3.1 OpenAI API Integration

OpenAI's API provides a range of tools for integrating powerful models like GPT-4 into your applications. By offering a REST API, OpenAI allows developers to send prompts to the model and receive generated outputs without needing to understand the underlying machine learning code. Platforms like **Zapier**, **Bubble**, and **Pipedream** offer low-code solutions that integrate seamlessly with **OpenAI's API**.

**How to Use OpenAI in Low-Code Platforms:**

- **Sign Up for OpenAI:** Create an account on OpenAI and get API access. You'll receive an API key that allows you to make requests to the GPT-4 model.

- **Connect API to a Low-Code Platform:** On platforms like Zapier or Bubble, use their built-in integration feature to connect OpenAI's API. For example, you can send customer questions to GPT-4 via an API call and display the AI-generated response in a chatbot interface.

- **Design the Application:** Use drag-and-drop tools to design your app's user interface, such as text input fields for prompts and output boxes for the AI's responses.

### 10.3.2 Bubble

Bubble is one of the most popular low-code development platforms, allowing users to build web applications from scratch using a visual editor. It supports API integrations, making it a perfect fit for incorporating AI models. Bubble provides workflows, which are automated sequences that dictate how the app responds to user inputs, making it easy to connect with AI services like OpenAI.

**Use Cases for Bubble:**

- **Build a customer support chatbot using OpenAI's GPT-4 that responds to user queries automatically.**

- **Create an AI-based recommendation engine that suggests products or services based on user preferences.**

- **Develop a text summarization tool that processes and summarizes large documents.**

### 10.3.3 Microsoft Power Platform

Microsoft Power Platform is a suite of low-code tools that includes Power Apps, Power Automate, and Power Virtual Agents. These platforms allow users to create AI-powered applications and workflows within the Microsoft ecosystem, making it a valuable tool for businesses already using tools like Azure and Microsoft 365.

**AI Capabilities of Power Platform:**

- **Power Apps:** Build AI-driven mobile or web applications using drag-and-drop functionality.

- **Power Automate:** Automate workflows with AI enhancements, such as sentiment analysis or data extraction from documents.

- **Power Virtual Agents:** Create AI-powered chatbots without writing any code, capable of handling customer inquiries, automating responses, and integrating with other business processes.

### 10.3.4 No-Code AI Solutions

There are also specific no-code platforms tailored for AI-based applications, **such as:**

- **Lobe:** A no-code AI platform by Microsoft designed to make machine learning model training simple and intuitive. Lobe uses visual examples to train models, ideal for image recognition tasks.

- **Teachable Machine:** A Google service that allows you to train custom machine learning models using a simple interface, useful for tasks like recognizing gestures or sound patterns.

## 10.4 Building a Low-Code AI Application: A Step-by-Step Guide

Let's explore how to build a low-code AI application using Bubble as an example. This walkthrough will cover the basics of setting up an app that leverages the power of GPT-4 to generate text based on user input.

### 10.4.1 Step 1: Create a Bubble Account

Visit **Bubble**.io and create a free account. Once you're in the dashboard, you can start a new project. Choose a template or begin from scratch depending on your needs.

### 10.4.2 Step 2: Design the Interface

Using Bubble's visual editor, design the user interface for your application. You can drag and drop elements **such as:**

• **Input Fields:** For users to enter their prompts or questions.

• **Buttons:** To trigger the AI to generate a response.

• **Output Boxes:** Where the AI's generated text will be displayed.

### 10.4.3 Step 3: Set Up Workflows

Workflows in Bubble define how the application behaves when users interact with it. For instance, when a user clicks the "Submit" button after entering a prompt, a workflow can be created to send this prompt to the OpenAI API and return a generated response.

• **Create a new workflow that triggers when the "Submit" button is clicked.**

• **Add an API Call to the workflow to send the user's input to OpenAI's GPT-4 model.**

- **Display the generated text in the designated output box.**

### 10.4.4 Step 4: Connect OpenAI's API

- **Bubble has an API Connector that allows you to integrate external APIs easily:**

- **Go to the Bubble plugin store and install the API Connector.**

- **Configure the API Connector with your OpenAI API key.**

- **Set up a new API call for GPT-4, including headers and the request body where the prompt will be passed.**

### 10.4.5 Step 5: Test and Deploy

Once the API is connected, and the workflows are set up, test the app by entering text prompts and viewing the AI-generated results. When you're satisfied, you can deploy the app, making it accessible to users.

### 10.5 Real-World Applications of Low-Code AI

Low-code AI platforms have real-world applications across **various sectors:**

### 10.5.1 Customer Service

AI-powered chatbots and virtual assistants built with low-code tools help companies streamline customer support. By integrating AI models like GPT-4, businesses can automate responses to customer inquiries, provide product recommendations, and even troubleshoot technical issues.

### 10.5.2 E-Commerce

Low-code platforms enable the creation of recommendation engines, where AI suggests products or services based on customer preferences. By analyzing user behavior and past interactions, businesses can deliver personalized shopping experiences.

### 10.5.3 Content Creation

Low-code AI applications are increasingly used for automating content generation. Whether it's generating product descriptions, social media posts, or blog articles, AI tools can save hours of manual work.

### 10.5.4 Healthcare

In healthcare, AI applications built with low-code tools help in medical data analysis, patient interaction automation, and even assisting doctors with diagnoses by analyzing large datasets or medical records.

### 10.6 Conclusion

Low-code AI platforms are revolutionizing how applications are built, making it easier for businesses and individuals to harness the power of AI without deep technical expertise.

By using platforms like Bubble, Power Platform, or Lobe, you can develop AI-driven solutions that enhance customer experiences, automate tasks, and deliver personalized services. Whether you're a developer looking to speed up the development process or a non-technical business owner wanting to build AI-powered apps, these tools provide a path toward innovation without complexity.

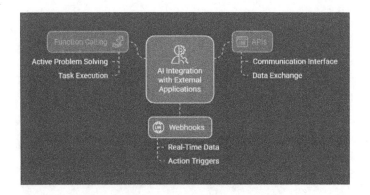

## 11.1 Introduction to AI Integration with External Applications

In the modern era of artificial intelligence (AI), models like GPT-4 have advanced from simply generating text to becoming capable of performing tasks by interacting with external applications. This interaction is made possible through function calling, APIs (Application Programming Interfaces), and webhooks, allowing AI to execute a broader range of tasks such as sending emails, retrieving real-time data, or even controlling IoT devices.

Function calling transforms AI from a passive tool to an active problem solver, integrating seamlessly with various platforms and services. This chapter focuses on how developers can use APIs and function calling to extend the capabilities of AI models, enabling them to perform real-world functions and become integrated into practical applications.

## 11.2 Understanding Function Calling in AI

Function calling is a method that allows AI to interact with external applications by invoking predefined functions or APIs. These functions are small, modular pieces of code that perform specific tasks, such as fetching data from a database, sending an email, or updating a user interface.

When AI integrates with external applications, it no longer merely generates text in response to a prompt but can trigger actions based on the user's needs. For instance, an AI chatbot might not just offer information but also perform actions like scheduling appointments, initiating payments, or pulling in real-time information from an external database.

**Key Components of Function Calling:**

- **Functions:** Defined actions that the AI can trigger, such as retrieving weather data or placing an order.

- **Arguments:** Inputs that are passed to functions to customize their behavior (e.g., location for weather data).

- **Return Values:** Outputs returned by the function after execution (e.g., weather report or order confirmation).

**11.3 APIs: The Backbone of AI Functionality**

An API (**Application Programming Interface**) is a software intermediary that allows two applications to communicate with each other. When integrating AI models with external applications, APIs act as the bridge that connects the AI with external systems, enabling it to execute actions beyond text generation.

For example, an e-commerce application might use an API to integrate with AI, allowing customers to check the status of an order by interacting with a chatbot. In this scenario, the AI model sends the request to an API, which retrieves the necessary information and passes it back to the user.

**How APIs Work:**

- **Request:** The AI sends a request to the API, specifying the action it wants to perform (e.g., fetching user data).

- **Processing:** The API processes the request and interacts with the backend system to retrieve the necessary data.

- **Response:** The API sends the requested data back to the AI, which can either display it to the user or perform further actions.

**Popular APIs for AI Integration:**

- **Twilio API:** For sending SMS, making calls, and managing customer communication.

- **Stripe API:** For processing payments and managing transactions.

- **Google Maps API:** For integrating location services, distance calculations, and routing.

- **OpenWeatherMap API:** For retrieving weather data.

### 11.4 Webhooks: Triggering Events in Real Time

**Webhooks** are another important concept in AI integration, allowing external applications to send real-time data to an AI model or other systems. Unlike APIs, which require the AI to actively send a request to retrieve information, webhooks allow applications to automatically send data to the AI model when specific events occur.

For example, when a new order is placed in an e-commerce store, a webhook could be triggered to send the order details to the AI-powered system, which could then generate a confirmation message or initiate further actions like shipment tracking.

**Key Advantages of Webhooks:**

- **Real-Time Communication:** Webhooks enable instant updates without needing the AI to repeatedly check for changes.

- **Efficiency:** Webhooks reduce the need for constant polling, which can save resources and speed up application response times.

- **Automation:** They enable seamless automation of tasks such as sending notifications or updating records.

**Real-World Use Cases of Webhooks:**

- **Payment Confirmation:** Webhooks send instant notifications to the AI system when a payment is completed, enabling immediate order fulfillment.

- **Issue Tracking:** Webhooks alert the AI system when a new issue is reported on a bug-tracking platform, allowing for automatic assignment or response.

- **Customer Support:** Webhooks notify customer service AI systems when a new ticket is created, allowing them to provide immediate assistance or escalate issues.

**11.5 Building AI Applications with Function Calling**

Let's walk through a step-by-step guide to building an AI application that integrates function calling to perform external tasks. In this example, we'll build a chatbot that retrieves real-time weather data using the *OpenWeatherMap API.*

### 11.5.1 Step 1: Choose an AI Platform

To implement function calling, start by choosing an AI platform that supports API integration. For instance:

**OpenAI API:** Allows you to interact with GPT-4 and execute function calls.

**Dialogflow:** A Google Cloud-based platform for building conversational agents with function calling features.

### 11.5.2 Step 2: Define the Function

For this example, we'll define a function that retrieves the weather for a given city. This function will make an API call to the OpenWeatherMap API, and the AI model will trigger it based on user input.

### 11.5.3 Step 3: Set Up API Integration

*1. Create an OpenWeatherMap account and get your API key.*

*2. Connect the API to your AI platform. For instance, if you're using OpenAI's API, you can set up the request to the weather API whenever a user asks for a weather update.*

*3. Pass Arguments: The function call will require the user to specify a city name, which will be passed as an argument to the API request.*

### 11.5.4 Step 4: Implement the Workflow

When the user asks, *"What's the weather in New York?":*

- The AI model recognizes the request and triggers the weather function.

- The weather function sends a request to the OpenWeatherMap API, passing "New York" as the argument.

- The API returns the current weather data, which is processed by the function and sent back to the user via the AI.

### 11.5.5 Step 5: Test and Optimize

Test the system to ensure it's returning accurate weather data and refine the user prompts to make the interaction as seamless as possible.

### 11.6 Real-World Applications of Function Calling in AI

AI models with function calling capabilities are being used in a wide range of industries to enhance efficiency, automate tasks, and provide better user experiences. Some key applications include:

### 11.6.1 Healthcare

AI chatbots in healthcare can integrate with hospital databases to book appointments, retrieve patient records, and offer personalized medical advice based on real-time health data.

### 11.6.2 E-Commerce

E-commerce platforms use AI to track orders, manage inventory, and process returns, all of which are made possible through APIs and function calling.

### 11.6.3 Finance

Banks and fintech companies integrate AI with financial systems to automate tasks such as balance inquiries, transaction processing, and fraud detection using real-time APIs.

### 11.6.4 Home Automation

Smart home systems integrate AI models to control devices, adjust thermostats, and monitor security systems, all using function calling to communicate with IoT devices.

## 11.7 Best Practices for Integrating AI with External Applications

When integrating AI models with external systems using function calling, it's important to follow certain best practices to ensure efficiency, security, and reliability.

### 11.7.1 API Rate Limiting

Most APIs have limits on how many requests can be made within a certain period. Ensure that your AI models are programmed to respect these limits, or you may risk overloading the API or being blocked.

### 11.7.2 Error Handling

API calls don't always succeed. It's crucial to implement error-handling mechanisms so that your AI knows how to respond when an API call fails. This could involve retrying the request, providing a fallback response to the user, or logging the error for later troubleshooting. A graceful failure ensures the AI application continues functioning smoothly, even in less-than-ideal circumstances.

### 11.7.3 Secure API Usage

When integrating external applications, always prioritize security. Make sure sensitive data such as API keys are stored securely and encrypted. Ensure that your AI model adheres to secure data transmission protocols, such as using HTTPS for all API requests. Additionally, set permissions and access controls to prevent unauthorized use of external APIs.

### 11.7.4 Monitoring and Logging

Regularly monitor the interactions between your AI model and external systems. Set up logging mechanisms to track API requests and responses, which helps in debugging and analyzing system performance. Monitoring also helps you anticipate potential system issues before they affect users.

### 11.8 Conclusion:

### Unlocking AI's Full Potential with Function Calling

Integrating external applications with AI through function calling unlocks a world of possibilities. From streamlining business operations to enhancing user experiences, this integration allows AI to go beyond passive interactions and perform real-world tasks that offer tangible benefits. Whether you're building customer support chatbots, automating workflows, or developing interactive AI applications, understanding how to implement function calling will be a critical skill in the future of AI development.

In the next chapter, we will explore the design considerations for AI applications, delving into how you can create user-friendly and engaging interfaces while ensuring the technology delivers its full potential in a secure and efficient manner.

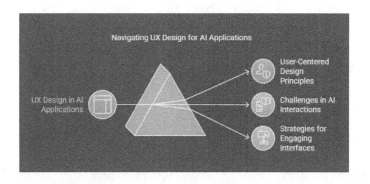

## 12.1 Introduction to UX in AI Applications

**User Experience (UX)** design is critical in any application, but when it comes to AI-powered systems, designing an intuitive and user-friendly interface becomes even more essential. AI applications interact dynamically with users, often offering complex and context-dependent functionality. As a result, crafting a seamless experience requires understanding both the technical complexities of AI and the needs of the user.

This chapter delves into the nuances of designing UX for AI applications, guiding you through the principles of user-centered design, addressing the challenges specific to AI interactions, and providing strategies for creating engaging, easy-to-use interfaces.

## 12.2 Key Principles of AI UX Design

Designing an AI application involves integrating predictive, generative, or decision-making capabilities into an interface that users can easily understand and interact with. Here are some core principles that will guide the design process:

### 12.2.1 Simplicity and Clarity

AI applications often perform complex tasks behind the scenes. As a designer, it's crucial to keep the interface as simple and intuitive as possible. Avoid overwhelming users with technical jargon or unnecessary features. Present information and actions clearly, using familiar design patterns that make the AI's capabilities easy to understand.

### 12.2.2 Transparency

AI systems often operate in ways that are not immediately apparent to users. It's essential to maintain a level of transparency in your design, so users understand why and how the AI is making decisions. This transparency builds trust and ensures users feel in control. For example, when an AI system offers a suggestion, it's helpful to include a short explanation of the reasoning behind the suggestion.

### 12.2.3 Feedback and Control

AI can sometimes make unpredictable decisions or generate results that aren't immediately helpful. In these instances, it's critical to provide users with feedback loops and controls. Allow users to correct AI actions or refine prompts, so they don't feel locked into a specific outcome. This empowers users to guide the AI towards better results and creates a more satisfying experience.

### 12.2.4 Personalization

One of AI's greatest strengths is its ability to offer personalized experiences based on user behavior and preferences. Tailor your application's interface to individual users, offering recommendations, prompts, or insights that are relevant to them. This can include customizing the visual layout, providing personalized suggestions, or adapting the interaction flow based on the user's previous choices.

## 12.3 Designing for Different AI Use Cases

AI applications vary widely in their use cases, and the UX design should reflect the type of interaction users will have with the AI system. Below are common AI use cases and tips for designing their interfaces:

### 12.3.1 Conversational AI (Chatbots)

For conversational AI systems like chatbots, the focus should be on creating a natural dialogue that mimics human interactions. Use simple, intuitive input fields for users to type their queries, and ensure the chatbot responds quickly with concise, understandable replies. Incorporate clarifying questions when the AI is unsure of the user's intent, and provide quick response buttons to help guide users through common workflows.

### 12.3.2 Predictive Analytics

AI applications used for predictive analytics must clearly communicate predictions, insights, and data. Use visual elements like charts, graphs, or progress bars to show predictions, probabilities, or recommendations in a digestible format. Additionally, ensure that users understand the data that led to the prediction by offering explorable, layered information that can go from simple overviews to more detailed reports.

### 12.3.3 Image and Video Generation

For AI-powered image or video generation applications, offer an intuitive workspace where users can provide prompts and see real-time previews of the AI-generated media. Include controls for users to refine their input and offer suggestions for prompt creation to guide users toward the best possible outcomes. Ensure easy access to download and share functions, as these are key to media-related applications.

### 12.3.4 Text Generation Tools

When designing a text generation tool like a writing assistant, focus on streamlining the process of generating and editing content. Offer users clear editing tools that allow them to quickly make changes to AI-generated text. Provide examples or prompt suggestions to help users formulate queries more effectively and include undo or redo functionality to give them more control over the content creation process.

### 12.4 Handling Technical Complexity with Usability

AI applications often rely on complex algorithms, data structures, and machine learning models. While these technical aspects are crucial for the system's functionality, the goal of UX design is to shield the user from unnecessary complexity. Below are key strategies for achieving this balance:

### 12.4.1 Layered Information Architecture

Offer users information in layers, starting with the most important and actionable insights first, and allowing users to drill down into more detailed data as needed. For example, a stock market prediction app should show users whether the market is trending up or down, and allow them to click for more detailed data and explanations if desired.

### 12.4.2 Progressive Disclosure

Rather than presenting all available features and options up front, use progressive disclosure to reveal complexity only when needed. For example, in an AI-powered design tool, provide basic editing controls first, and only introduce advanced features like layering, color blending, or texture generation when the user requests them.

### 12.4.3 Guided Interaction

Guided interaction helps reduce the cognitive load on users, making the AI system easier to use. Offer tutorials, tooltips, and guided workflows that help users understand how to interact with the AI model and achieve their goals. For instance, in an AI-based video editing tool, a brief guide showing how to apply filters or add transitions can dramatically improve the user experience.

### 12.4.4 Error Handling

Since AI systems don't always deliver perfect results, it's essential to design for error handling. Whether it's an incorrect response from a chatbot or a poorly generated image, provide users with clear ways to fix mistakes, ask for new results, or revert to earlier states. A helpful error message that explains why something went wrong and what users can do next is much better than simply displaying an error code.

### 12.5 Creating Engaging Visual Design for AI Applications

Visual design plays a significant role in creating an engaging user experience. For AI applications, the interface should not only look appealing but also facilitate easy interaction with the system's advanced capabilities. Here are some visual design considerations:

### 12.5.1 Minimalism and Clarity

AI applications often handle complex data and interactions. A minimalist design with a clear layout helps users focus on the essential parts of the interface without feeling overwhelmed. Use whitespace, simple icons, and concise text to guide users through the application's features.

### 12.5.2 Visual Cues for AI Interaction

When interacting with AI, users need visual feedback to confirm that the system is processing their request. For instance, a progress bar or animated icon can show that the AI is generating a response. These cues help manage user expectations and reduce frustration when there are delays.

### 12.5.3 Data Visualization

AI applications often involve large datasets, and proper data visualization is essential for making this information understandable. Use graphs, charts, and interactive elements to present AI-generated data in a way that is both informative and aesthetically pleasing. Allow users to manipulate the data to explore different aspects without needing advanced technical skills.

### 12.5.4 Customization Options

Offer users the ability to customize the interface to suit their needs. This could include changing themes (light/dark mode), adjusting the layout of data panels, or even personalizing the AI model's behavior based on previous interactions. Giving users control over how they interact with the system enhances the overall experience and satisfaction.

### 12.6 Balancing AI Automation and Human Input

When designing AI applications, one of the biggest challenges is finding the right balance between automation and human input. Too much automation can make users feel out of control, while too little negates the power of AI. Striking this balance ensures that users feel both empowered and supported by the AI system.

### 12.6.1 Offering Control Options

Allow users to toggle between automated and manual control. For example, in an AI-powered image editing tool, let users choose between fully automated adjustments or manual controls where they can tweak each setting. Offering both options ensures that users feel comfortable with the level of automation.

### 12.6.2 Human-AI Collaboration

Design the system to encourage human-AI collaboration, where the AI assists in tasks but does not completely take over. For example, in a writing assistant, allow the AI to suggest improvements, but give the user final control over the edits.

### 12.7 Conclusion: Crafting Seamless UX for AI Applications

Designing for AI applications requires a unique blend of understanding both technology and human behavior. By focusing on simplicity, transparency, and control, you can create user-friendly interfaces that make interacting with AI intuitive and enjoyable. Whether you're building chatbots, predictive tools, or image generation apps, the goal is to create a seamless experience where AI enhances user productivity while staying out of the way.

As you move forward in designing AI applications, remember that good UX ensures the AI's power is accessible without overwhelming the user. Balancing technical complexity with usability is key to building products that people will love to use. In the next chapter, we will dive into securing generative AI applications and ensuring data privacy and compliance with ethical standards.

# SECURING YOUR GENERATIVE AI APPLICATIONS

## 13.1 Introduction to AI Security

As generative AI applications become increasingly prevalent, ensuring their security has become a critical concern for developers and organizations. These applications often handle sensitive user data, engage in complex decision-making processes, and can be targets for malicious actors. Securing generative AI systems involves a multi-faceted approach that encompasses protecting user data, preventing unauthorized access, and safeguarding against vulnerabilities.

This chapter will explore the key aspects of securing generative AI applications, emphasizing best practices, potential threats, and strategies to create robust security measures.

## 13.2 Understanding the Threat Landscape

To effectively secure generative AI applications, it's crucial to understand the types of threats they may face. These include:

### 13.2.1 Data Breaches

Data breaches can occur when unauthorized individuals gain access to sensitive user information, which can lead to identity theft, fraud, and other malicious activities. Given that generative AI applications often process large amounts of data, the risk of data exposure is significant.

### 13.2.2 Model Inversion Attacks

Model inversion attacks involve adversaries trying to reconstruct sensitive data from the outputs of an AI model. For example, if a generative model produces realistic text or images based on user input, an attacker could analyze these outputs to infer the original data used to train the model, potentially exposing private information.

### 13.2.3 Adversarial Attacks

Generative AI applications are susceptible to adversarial attacks, where malicious inputs are designed to deceive the model. These inputs can manipulate the model's outputs, resulting in incorrect or harmful responses. For instance, an attacker could craft a deceptive prompt to generate inappropriate content.

### 13.2.4 Denial of Service (DoS) Attacks

Denial of Service attacks aim to overwhelm an application, rendering it unavailable to legitimate users. For AI applications that rely on cloud-based resources, such attacks can disrupt service and affect user trust.

### 13.3 Key Principles of AI Security

Developing a robust security framework for generative AI applications requires adherence to key principles that ensure both data protection and application integrity.

### 13.3.1 Data Protection and Privacy

Protecting user data is paramount. This involves implementing encryption techniques, both for data at rest and in transit. Data encryption ensures that even if data is intercepted or accessed without authorization, it remains unreadable without the proper decryption keys.

**Best Practices:**

Use industry-standard encryption protocols (e.g., AES-256 for data at rest).
Implement HTTPS for secure data transmission.
Regularly audit data access logs to identify unauthorized access attempts.

### 13.3.2 Access Control

Implementing strict access controls is essential to prevent unauthorized access to your AI applications. This involves defining user roles and permissions to ensure that only authorized personnel can access sensitive functions or data.

**Best Practices:**

Use role-based access control (**RBAC**) to define permissions based on user roles.

Implement multi-factor authentication (MFA) to enhance user verification.

Regularly review and update access controls to align with changing user roles.

### 13.3.3 Monitoring and Logging

Continuous monitoring and logging are critical for detecting and responding to security incidents. Monitoring tools can help identify unusual patterns of behavior, such as unauthorized access attempts or unexpected model outputs.

**Best Practices:**

Implement real-time monitoring solutions that provide alerts for suspicious activities.

Maintain detailed logs of user interactions with the AI system for forensic analysis.

Regularly review logs to identify potential security vulnerabilities.

### 13.4 Protecting Against Specific Threats

### 13.4.1 Guarding Against Data Breaches

To minimize the risk of data breaches, it is crucial to adopt a data minimization approach, ensuring that only the necessary data is collected and retained. Additionally, organizations should implement strong data governance policies to enforce compliance with privacy regulations.

**Best Practices:**

Limit the collection of personal data to what is strictly necessary for the application's functionality.

Regularly assess data storage practices to ensure compliance with regulations such as GDPR or CCPA.

Conduct regular vulnerability assessments and penetration testing to identify and address weaknesses.

### 13.4.2 Mitigating Model Inversion Risks

To reduce the risk of model inversion attacks, consider employing techniques such as differential privacy, which adds noise to the model's outputs to obscure individual data points.

**Best Practices:**

Implement differential privacy measures during model training to protect sensitive training data.

Regularly update your models to minimize the impact of exposed data.

### 13.4.3 Defending Against Adversarial Attacks

Developing a robust defense against adversarial attacks involves training your models to recognize and handle malicious inputs. Techniques such as adversarial training can enhance a model's resilience.

**Best Practices:**

Use adversarial training techniques to expose your models to potential attacks during training.

Monitor model outputs for unexpected or harmful content, and implement safeguards to mitigate risks.

### 13.4.4 Preventing Denial of Service Attacks

Implementing rate limiting and traffic management strategies can help protect against DoS attacks by controlling the flow of requests to your application.

**Best Practices:**

Use rate limiting to restrict the number of requests a user can make within a specified time frame.

Implement load balancing to distribute traffic evenly across servers, minimizing the impact of an attack.

## 13.5 Building a Security Culture

Security is not solely the responsibility of the IT team; it requires a holistic approach that involves all stakeholders within the organization. Building a security-aware culture is essential for ensuring that everyone understands their role in maintaining security.

### 13.5.1 Employee Training and Awareness

Regular training sessions can educate employees about security risks and best practices. Employees should be aware of the importance of security protocols and how to recognize potential threats.

**Best Practices:**

Conduct regular security awareness training for all employees.

Include simulated phishing attacks to test employees' responses and raise awareness.

### 13.5.2 Establishing a Security Incident Response Plan

Organizations should develop a comprehensive security incident response plan outlining procedures for responding to security breaches or attacks. This plan should include roles, responsibilities, and communication protocols to ensure a swift and coordinated response.

**Best Practices:**

Regularly review and update the incident response plan to incorporate lessons learned from previous incidents.

Conduct tabletop exercises to test the effectiveness of the plan and identify areas for improvement.

## 13.6 Conclusion: Prioritizing Security in AI Development

As generative AI applications continue to evolve and gain traction, the importance of security cannot be overstated. Implementing robust security measures that protect user data, prevent unauthorized access, and defend against vulnerabilities is crucial for building trust and ensuring the safe deployment of AI technologies.

By understanding the threat landscape, adhering to best practices, and fostering a security-conscious culture, organizations can create secure generative AI applications that harness the power of AI while safeguarding user interests.

In the next chapter, we will explore the generative AI application lifecycle, examining how to manage the development and deployment processes effectively to maximize the benefits of AI technologies.

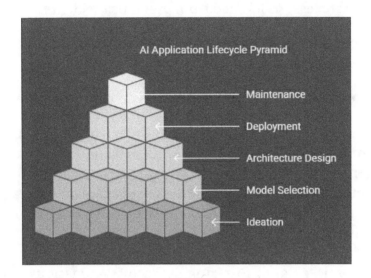

## 14.1 Introduction to the AI Application Life-cycle

Developing a generative AI application is a complex, multi-stage process that requires careful planning, execution, and ongoing maintenance. To create an application that is both effective and scalable, developers must navigate various phases, from ideation to model selection, through to deployment and post-launch maintenance. This chapter will explore the complete lifecycle of generative AI applications, offering insights into best practices at each stage to ensure your application grows in line with your business needs.

We'll cover key aspects such as:

Ideation and defining the use case

Selecting and training the right AI models

Application architecture and design

Deployment strategies

Monitoring, scaling, and maintaining the application

By understanding each phase of the lifecycle, you can create an AI application that delivers long-term value while being adaptable to future business challenges and opportunities.

## 14.2 Ideation: Defining the Use Case

Before diving into model selection or coding, it's essential to clearly define your AI application's use case. Ideation is about pinpointing the problem you want to solve or the value you wish to create with generative AI.

### 14.2.1 Identifying Business Goals

Your AI application must align with business goals. Whether you're automating customer service, generating creative content, or optimizing operations, clearly define the problem your application will address.

### Best Practices:

Conduct market research to identify demand for AI solutions in your field.

Collaborate with stakeholders (product managers, marketers, developers) to outline application objectives.

Create user personas to understand the end-user's needs and how AI can enhance their experience.

### 14.2.2 Understanding AI's Role

Not every problem requires AI, so it's important to evaluate if AI is the best solution for your use case. Generative AI excels at tasks like language generation, content creation, and automating repetitive processes.

**Key Considerations:**

Is the problem complex enough to require AI?

Can AI improve efficiency, accuracy, or creativity in ways traditional software cannot?

## 14.3 Model Selection: Choosing the Right Generative AI

Once you've defined the use case, the next step is selecting the appropriate model to power your AI application. Different generative models come with unique strengths and limitations, so it's critical to pick the right one based on your application's needs.

### 14.3.1 Pre-trained Models vs. Custom Models

Pre-trained models such as GPT-4 or DALL·E are popular choices for many generative applications because they offer powerful capabilities without requiring you to build a model from scratch. Alternatively, fine-tuning a pre-trained model on specific datasets may offer more customized solutions.

**Best Practices:**

Start with pre-trained models to save time and resources.

Fine-tune models to align them more closely with your specific use case (e.g., industry-specific language or style).

### 14.3.2 Selecting the Right API or Framework

Several AI APIs and frameworks can streamline model

integration. Tools like **OpenAI's API, Hugging Face**

**Transformers, and Google Cloud AI** offer robust environments for building applications.

**Key Frameworks:**

**OpenAI GPT:** Great for text-based applications like chatbots and content generation.

**DALL·E:** Ideal for image generation applications.

**Hugging Face Transformers:** A versatile library for experimenting with multiple types of AI models.

## 14.4 Application Architecture and Design

Once the model is selected, the next step is to define the architecture of the application. This involves outlining how the AI will interact with users, other systems, and databases. Designing an intuitive and efficient architecture is crucial for creating a scalable and responsive AI application.

### 14.4.1 Defining the Application Flow

At this stage, determine how the user interacts with your AI system. For example, in a chatbot application, consider how user inputs will be processed, how the model generates a response, and how that response will be displayed to the user.

**Best Practices:**

Map out the entire user flow, including how the AI interacts with databases, APIs, and user inputs.

Design systems that allow flexibility for future features or integrations.

### 14.4.2 Frontend and Backend Integration

For AI applications to function smoothly, frontend and backend systems must be tightly integrated. The backend (which includes the AI model, databases, and servers) processes user data, while the frontend provides a user-friendly interface.

**Key Considerations:**

Implement robust **API** layers to connect the AI model with user interfaces.

Ensure the backend architecture supports scaling as user demand increases.

## 14.5 Deployment Strategies: Scaling and Efficiency

Once the architecture is designed and the AI model is integrated, you're ready for deployment. This stage focuses on ensuring your AI application runs smoothly in a real-world environment. Deployment strategies involve selecting the right infrastructure and cloud services to run your AI model efficiently and at scale.

### 14.5.1 Cloud-based Deployment

Most generative AI applications rely on cloud services like AWS, Google Cloud, or Microsoft Azure for deployment. These platforms offer the scalability needed to handle large amounts of data and traffic.

**Best Practices:**

Use cloud orchestration tools like Kubernetes to automate deployment, scaling, and management.

Select cloud services that provide **GPU/TPU** support for AI models requiring high computational power.

### 14.5.2 Managing Resources

Efficient resource management is critical to keeping operational costs low while maintaining high performance. By dynamically scaling resources based on demand, you can ensure your

AI application remains responsive without overspending on infrastructure.

**Best Practices:**

Implement auto-scaling to dynamically adjust compute resources based on user demand.

Use monitoring tools (such as **AWS CloudWatch or Google Cloud Monitoring**) to track resource usage and application performance.

## 14.6 Maintenance and Continuous Improvement

After deployment, your AI application requires continuous maintenance and updates. Over time, as more users interact with the system, you'll gather valuable data that can be used to improve the model's accuracy and performance.

### 14.6.1 Monitoring and Logging

Regular monitoring ensures your application functions as expected. Logs can help identify issues such as model drift (when the model's predictions degrade over time due to changing input data) or slow response times.

**Best Practices:**

Implement real-time monitoring for critical components, including model predictions, response time, and user interactions.

Use logs to troubleshoot errors and refine the model as needed.

### 14.6.2 Updating and Retraining Models

As data changes, so should your model. Retraining ensures that your AI system remains relevant and accurate. For example, if you're using AI for customer service, retrain the model to reflect evolving customer queries and language patterns.

**Best Practices:**

Schedule regular intervals for model retraining (e.g., quarterly or semi-annually) based on new data.

Introduce A/B testing when implementing significant model updates to gauge their impact on performance.

### 14.6.3 Incorporating User Feedback

User feedback is a powerful tool for improving AI applications. Collect feedback on model responses, user satisfaction, and ease of use to continually refine your application.

**Best Practices:**

Provide users with an option to give feedback on AI-generated content.

Regularly update user interfaces based on feedback to enhance the overall user experience.

### 14.7 Conclusion: Building for the Future

The life-cycle of a generative AI application doesn't end at deployment. Successful applications require ongoing maintenance, updates, and scaling to meet user demands and business goals. By understanding each phase of the life-cycle —from ideation to continuous improvement—you can build robust, scalable AI systems that deliver lasting value.

In the next chapter, we will explore Retrieval Augmented Generation **(RAG)** and the role of vector databases in enhancing AI applications, delving into how these cutting-edge techniques can improve performance and capabilities.

# RETRIEVAL AUGMENTED GENERATION (RAG) AND VECTOR DATABASES

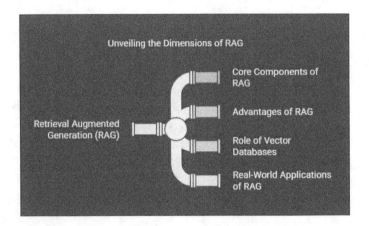

## 15.1 Introduction to Retrieval Augmented Generation (RAG)

In the fast-paced world of artificial intelligence, the need for generating precise and contextually accurate responses is paramount. While generative AI models like GPT-4 are incredibly powerful at generating text based on prompts, they sometimes struggle to provide information that is highly accurate or up-to-date. This is where Retrieval Augmented Generation **(RAG)** comes into play.

RAG is an advanced technique that combines the strengths of traditional search methods with generative AI. It allows AI models to retrieve relevant external information from a database or knowledge repository and then use that information to generate more informed, accurate, and reliable responses. By blending retrieval capabilities with generation, RAG enables AI systems to overcome the limitations of relying solely on pre-trained knowledge and enhances their ability to handle real-time information.

In this chapter, we will explore the core components of RAG, its advantages, and how vector databases enhance RAG systems. We will also look at real-world applications where RAG can revolutionize search and knowledge-based systems.

## 15.2 How RAG Works: The Integration of Retrieval and Generation

RAG enhances generative models by incorporating two critical steps: retrieval and generation.

### 15.2.1 The Retrieval Process

The first phase in a RAG system is retrieval. Instead of relying solely on the model's internal parameters for generating text, a RAG system searches for relevant pieces of information in external sources (e.g., documents, databases, or knowledge bases). This external information serves as a foundation for the model's output.

**In a typical RAG system:**

**1.** The AI receives a user query (input prompt).

**2.** The query is encoded into vector embeddings, a mathematical representation of the text that captures its meaning and context.

**3.** These embeddings are compared with a large database of pre-indexed documents or knowledge entries.

**4.** The most relevant documents or entries are retrieved based on similarity scores with the query.

## 15.2.2 The Generation Process

Once relevant information is retrieved, the generative model uses this additional context to generate an informed and accurate response. By augmenting the model's natural language generation abilities with real-time information, the final output is more precise and useful.

The main advantage here is that the generative AI is no longer confined to the knowledge it was trained on but can dynamically access and integrate new information, making it more powerful and adaptive.

## 15.3 The Role of Vector Databases in RAG

Central to the success of a RAG system is the use of vector databases, which allow the AI to efficiently search and retrieve relevant information from massive datasets. Vector databases store data in the form of vectors (embeddings), which makes it easy to compare and retrieve similar items based on the query.

## 15.3.1 What Are Vector Databases?

A vector database stores data as high-dimensional vectors instead of traditional relational or document-based storage systems. In these databases, each document, paragraph, or piece of knowledge is represented as a vector that captures the semantic meaning of the text. These vectors are produced using AI models like BERT, GPT, or other embedding models.

For example, if you have a document about "artificial intelligence in healthcare," it will be converted into a vector that encodes the semantic meaning of that document. When a query like "How is AI used in medical diagnosis?" is issued, the query will also be encoded as a vector and compared to all other vectors in the database. The closest matches (documents with similar meaning) will be retrieved.

### 15.3.2 Why Vector Databases?

Traditional databases excel at structured, tabular data. However, they struggle with unstructured data like text, images, or documents where the meaning isn't easily represented through rows and columns. Vector databases enable fast, accurate search across unstructured data by comparing semantic meanings rather than exact keyword matches.

**Some popular vector databases include:**

**Faiss (Facebook AI Similarity Search)**

**Pinecone**

**Milvus**

These databases are designed to handle massive amounts of vector data, making them ideal for large-scale AI applications that require high-performance retrieval.

### 15.4 RAG Use Cases: Revolutionizing Search and Knowledge Applications

RAG and vector databases are transforming various industries by improving the quality and efficiency of search and knowledge-based applications. Below, we'll discuss some key use cases.

### 15.4.1 Enhanced Search Engines

Traditional search engines rely heavily on keyword matching, which can result in irrelevant or outdated results. By integrating RAG, search engines can retrieve documents that are not just based on keyword presence but also on their relevance to the context of the query.

For instance, when searching for a legal precedent in a large corpus of legal documents, a RAG-powered search engine can retrieve highly relevant cases based on the specific context of the legal query, ensuring lawyers and researchers get the most applicable information.

### 15.4.2 Customer Support Systems

In customer support applications, RAG can provide accurate, real-time responses by retrieving relevant information from knowledge bases or FAQ documents and combining it with generative capabilities to create responses tailored to customer queries.

For example, in a tech support scenario, a RAG-based system can search a knowledge base for relevant troubleshooting articles while generating a personalized, step-by-step solution for the customer.

### 15.4.3 Educational Tools and Research

RAG can significantly improve tools designed for learning and research. For students and researchers, it can retrieve the most relevant study materials, research papers, or datasets and generate summaries or explanations based on the retrieved content. This improves both the quality and speed of knowledge acquisition.

### 15.4.4 Document Summarization

When dealing with large volumes of documents, summarization tools powered by RAG can retrieve key points from relevant sections of documents, allowing users to quickly get an overview of the content. For instance, a lawyer may use RAG to summarize a lengthy contract while ensuring that important legal clauses are highlighted.

## 15.5 Building a RAG-Powered AI System: Step-by-Step

Building a RAG system requires several key components, including embedding models, vector databases, and a generation model. Below is a simplified overview of how to construct such a system.

### 15.5.1 Step 1: Setting Up the Embedding Model

The first step is selecting and training an embedding model to convert text into vectors. Popular models for this task include BERT, GPT, and Sentence Transformers. The embedding model converts both the user's query and the knowledge base documents into vectors.

### 15.5.2 Step 2: Indexing Data into a Vector Database

Once you have the embeddings, they need to be indexed into a vector database like Faiss or Pinecone. This allows the system to perform fast similarity searches between the query and indexed documents.

### 15.5.3 Step 3: Implementing the Retrieval Mechanism

In this stage, the system is designed to search the vector database when a query is received. Based on the similarity scores, the top documents or information are retrieved for further processing.

### 15.5.4 Step 4: Generating a Response

The retrieved data is then fed into a generative model like GPT-4, which uses the context to generate a final response or output for the user.

### 15.5.5 Step 5: Testing and Refinement

Once your RAG system is set up, it's essential to test and refine it. Ensure that the retrieved documents and the generated responses are accurate, relevant, and aligned with user expectations.

### 15.6 Conclusion: The Future of AI-Powered Search and Knowledge Applications

**RAG** is a game-changer in the AI space, bringing together the best of both retrieval and generative capabilities. By leveraging vector databases and advanced embedding techniques, RAG systems can vastly improve search engines, customer support applications, research tools, and more.

As AI continues to evolve, we can expect RAG to play an even more critical role in how information is retrieved and presented, transforming the way we interact with data in both personal and professional settings.

In the next chapter, we will explore Open Source Models and Hugging Face, delving into how open-source tools and models are empowering developers to create sophisticated AI applications.

# OPEN SOURCE MODELS AND HUGGING FACE

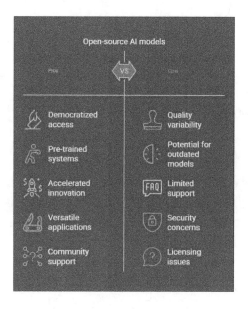

## 16.1 Introduction to Open-Source Models

The rise of open-source models has democratized access to advanced AI technologies, enabling developers, researchers, and even hobbyists to build sophisticated AI systems without needing to develop models from scratch. Open-source models are pre-trained AI systems that are freely available for anyone to use, modify, and fine-tune for specific tasks. The availability of these models has accelerated innovation, allowing individuals and organizations to quickly integrate AI into their applications.

One of the most significant platforms that has contributed to this movement is Hugging Face, a hub for open-source models, datasets, and machine learning tools. Hugging Face offers a large collection of pre-trained models that can be adapted for tasks ranging from natural language processing (NLP) to computer vision, making it a go-to resource for anyone looking to implement AI solutions.

In this chapter, we'll explore the advantages of using open-source models, highlight some popular models available on Hugging Face, and explain how you can fine-tune these models to meet specific project requirements. We will also dive into the tools and resources Hugging Face offers that make it easier to experiment and deploy AI systems.

## 16.2 The Benefits of Open-Source AI Models

### 16.2.1 Cost-Effective Development

Developing an AI model from scratch requires significant computational resources and expertise. Open-source models eliminate this barrier by providing pre-trained systems that are ready to use. This drastically reduces development time and costs, allowing even small teams to leverage the power of AI.

### 16.2.2 Easy Customization

Open-source models are typically designed with flexibility in mind, allowing users to fine-tune them for specific tasks. For instance, if you need a model for sentiment analysis but want it to be tailored to financial data, you can fine-tune an existing pre-trained model instead of training a new one from scratch.

### 16.2.3 Large Community Support

One of the greatest advantages of open-source models is the active community behind them. With millions of developers using and improving these models, there's a wealth of tutorials, documentation, and pre-built components that make it easy to integrate and modify these models according to your needs. You can tap into forums and repositories like GitHub to seek help or contribute to the development of these tools.

### 16.2.4 Constant Innovation

The open-source nature of these models means they are constantly being updated with the latest advancements in AI. This ensures that you always have access to cutting-edge technology, which is particularly important in the fast-moving world of machine learning.

### 16.3 Hugging Face: A Hub for Open-Source AI

Hugging Face has emerged as one of the leading platforms for open-source AI models, particularly in the area of natural language processing (**NLP**). It offers thousands of models that can perform tasks such as text classification, translation, summarization, and more. However, Hugging Face is not limited to **NLP**. It also provides models for speech, vision, and multimodal tasks.

### 16.3.1 The Hugging Face Model Hub

The Hugging Face Model Hub is an online repository where developers can find pre-trained models that cover a wide range of tasks. The Model Hub is structured in a way that makes it easy to search for models by task, framework, or model architecture. For example, you can find models based on BERT, GPT, and other popular architectures, each of which has been fine-tuned for specific use cases.

**Some widely used models on Hugging Face include:**

**BERT:** A model for tasks like question answering and text classification.

**GPT-2 and GPT-3:** For tasks like text generation, summarization, and translation.

**T5:** A versatile model that can handle translation, summarization, and other NLP tasks.

Each model comes with detailed documentation, including instructions on how to use, fine-tune, and deploy the model. Many models also provide a live demo, allowing users to test the model directly from the browser before downloading or integrating it into their projects.

### 16.3.2 The Hugging Face Transformers Library

The Hugging Face Transformers library is a powerful tool for working with pre-trained models. It provides easy access to state-of-the-art models in just a few lines of code. The library supports a wide range of tasks, including text generation, token classification, and sequence classification.

Here's an example of how easy it is to use the Transformers library to load a pre-trained model:

```
from transformers import pipeline

# Load a pre-trained text generation model
generator = pipeline('text-generation', model='gpt2')

# Generate text
response = generator("The future of AI is", max_length=50)
print(response)
```

This simplicity makes Hugging Face's tools accessible even to developers with limited experience in AI, as it abstracts away much of the complexity involved in working with machine learning models.

### 16.3.3 Datasets and Tools

Hugging Face also offers an extensive library of datasets that can be used to train or fine-tune models. These datasets cover a variety of fields, including text, speech, and vision, and are easily accessible through Hugging Face's Datasets library.

In addition to datasets, Hugging Face offers tools like Tokenizers for efficient text processing and Accelerate for optimizing model training and deployment across different hardware configurations. These tools make it easier to fine-tune and deploy models at scale.

### 16.4 Fine-Tuning Open-Source Models

Fine-tuning is the process of taking a pre-trained model and adapting it to a specific task or dataset. While pre-trained models are useful for many general tasks, fine-tuning allows you to achieve higher accuracy and performance on domain-specific tasks.

### 16.4.1 Why Fine-Tune Models?

While pre-trained models have learned a wide range of patterns from vast datasets, they may not always perform optimally on your specific use case. For example, a general-purpose language model might not understand the nuances of legal or medical text. Fine-tuning allows you to train the model on your dataset, improving its ability to generate relevant and accurate outputs.

### 16.4.2 Fine-Tuning with Hugging Face

Hugging Face makes it easy to fine-tune models using its Transformers library. The process typically involves:

**1. Loading a Pre-trained Model:** Select a base model from the Hugging Face Model Hub.

**2.Preparing Your Dataset:** Organize your dataset into the required format (e.g., text classification, summarization).

**3.Training:** Use the provided tools to train the model on your specific dataset.

**4.Evaluation and Deployment:** Evaluate the model's performance and deploy it to your application.

*Here's an example of fine-tuning a BERT model for text classification:*

```
from transformers import BertForSequenceClassification, Trainer, TrainingArguments

# Load a pre-trained BERT model for sequence classification
model = BertForSequenceClassification.from_pretrained('bert-base-uncased', num_labels=2)

# Define training arguments
training_args = TrainingArguments(
    output_dir='./results',
    learning_rate=2e-5,
    per_device_train_batch_size=16,
    num_train_epochs=3,
)

# Load your dataset and train the model
trainer = Trainer(
    model=model,
    args=training_args,
    train_dataset=train_dataset,
    eval_dataset=eval_dataset,
)

trainer.train()
```

With a few lines of code, you can fine-tune a model and integrate it into your application.

### 16.5 The Future of Open-Source AI

The open-source model ecosystem, led by platforms like Hugging Face, is continuously evolving. As more developers contribute models and tools, the diversity and capability of open-source AI solutions will only increase. The future promises models that are not only more powerful but also more accessible, enabling innovation across industries.

Whether you're building an AI-driven chatbot, a personalized recommendation system, or a medical diagnosis assistant, open-source models provide the foundation you need to succeed.

In the next chapter, we will explore AI Agents, autonomous systems that can perform tasks and make decisions on their own, expanding the capabilities of AI even further.

By leveraging open-source models and tools from Hugging Face, developers of all skill levels can accelerate their AI projects, bringing powerful AI solutions to life quickly and efficiently.

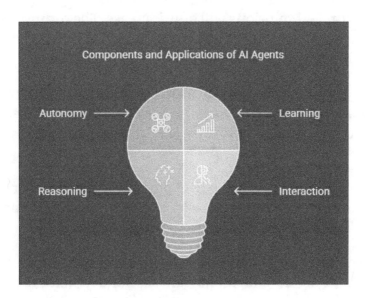

## 17.1 Introduction to AI Agents

AI agents are autonomous programs designed to perform tasks, make decisions, and interact with the environment without requiring constant user input. Unlike traditional software, which executes predefined instructions, AI agents can learn from their environment, adapt to new conditions, and act independently to achieve specified goals. These agents can solve real-world problems, manage complex workflows, and operate in dynamic environments, making them invaluable in industries ranging from customer service to robotics.

The concept of AI agents is rooted in several key principles of artificial intelligence:

- **Autonomy:** The ability to operate independently without continuous intervention.

- **Learning:** The capacity to learn from experience and improve performance over time.

- **Reasoning:** The ability to make decisions based on available information and logic.

- **Interaction:** Engaging with humans or other systems to accomplish tasks.

In this chapter, we'll explore the basics of AI agents, their applications, and how they are built and trained. We'll also examine the challenges involved in creating AI agents and some practical use cases.

## 17.2 Types of AI Agents

There are different types of AI agents, each designed to handle specific tasks or environments. The most common classifications include:

### 17.2.1 Reactive Agents

Reactive agents are the simplest form of AI agents. They respond to environmental stimuli and make decisions based on predefined rules or patterns. These agents do not possess memory or learning capabilities; they operate purely on current inputs. An example of a reactive agent is a chatbot programmed to respond to customer queries based on keyword matching.

**Use Case:** A simple customer service chatbot that provides automated responses to frequently asked questions **(FAQs).**

### 17.2.2 Model-Based Agents

Model-based agents have an internal representation of their environment, which allows them to reason and plan. These agents can predict future states based on their current actions, making them more versatile than reactive agents. They are capable of handling more complex tasks and interacting with dynamic environments.

Use Case: A recommendation engine that suggests products based on user behavior and preferences, using past interactions to guide future recommendations.

### 17.2.3 Goal-Oriented Agents

Goal-oriented agents are designed to achieve specific goals, often using advanced planning techniques. They can balance multiple objectives and evaluate various strategies to optimize their actions. These agents are commonly used in industries that require complex decision-making, such as supply chain management or financial trading.

**Use Case:** A supply chain management system that autonomously adjusts orders and inventory based on demand predictions and cost optimization.

### 17.2.4 Learning Agents

Learning agents are the most advanced type, capable of learning from their experiences and improving their performance over time. These agents use machine learning techniques, such as reinforcement learning, to adapt to new situations and environments. They are ideal for dynamic and uncertain environments where predefined rules may not be effective.

**Use Case:** An autonomous vehicle that learns how to navigate new cities by analyzing real-time traffic data and environmental conditions.

### 17.3 Building AI Agents

Building an AI agent requires integrating several AI technologies, including machine learning, natural language processing **(NLP)**, computer vision, and robotics. The process generally involves the following steps:

### 17.3.1 Defining the Agent's Goal

The first step in building an AI agent is to define the goal it is meant to achieve. Whether the agent's objective is to assist customers, make predictions, or solve a problem, a clear goal helps guide the development process.

**Example:** Building an AI agent to provide customer support by answering complex queries and escalating unresolved issues to human operators.

### 17.3.2 Creating an Environment

The environment is the space in which the AI agent operates. This could be a physical environment, such as a warehouse or factory, or a virtual one, like a website or software system. The environment provides the inputs that the agent uses to make decisions, and it serves as the medium through which the agent acts to achieve its goals.

**Example:** An AI agent operating within a customer service software platform, accessing the database to provide relevant information to customers.

### 17.3.3 Training the Agent

Most AI agents, especially those using machine learning, require training to learn how to perform their tasks effectively. Training an agent typically involves using historical data, such as customer interactions, or real-time simulations where the agent can practice different actions and evaluate their outcomes.

**Training Methods:**

**Supervised Learning:** The agent is trained on labeled datasets where correct outcomes are provided.

**Reinforcement Learning:** The agent learns by interacting with its environment and receiving rewards or penalties based on its actions.

**Example:** Training a chatbot agent to handle various customer inquiries, using historical chat logs as training data.

### 17.3.4 Implementing Decision-Making Algorithms

The agent's ability to make decisions autonomously is driven by decision-making algorithms. These algorithms help the agent evaluate its current situation and decide on the best course of action. Common decision-making algorithms include rule-based systems, heuristic methods, and more complex neural networks for deep learning-based agents.

**Example:** A recommendation agent that uses a collaborative filtering algorithm to suggest products to users based on similar user preferences.

### 17.3.5 Deploying the Agent

Once the agent is trained and capable of making decisions, it can be deployed in the intended environment. Depending on the complexity of the agent, this might involve integrating the agent with software platforms, hardware systems, or other tools needed to facilitate interaction with the real world.

**Example:** Deploying a conversational AI agent on a website to assist with customer inquiries, seamlessly integrated into the company's CRM system.

## 17.4 Applications of AI Agents

AI agents have become integral to a wide range of industries. Here are some notable applications:

### 17.4.1 Autonomous Vehicles

Self-driving cars are among the most well-known examples of AI agents. These agents use a combination of computer vision, sensor data, and decision-making algorithms to navigate roads, obey traffic laws, and avoid obstacles.

### 17.4.2 Virtual Assistants

Virtual assistants like Siri, Alexa, and Google Assistant are AI agents designed to help users perform tasks through voice commands. These agents can manage calendars, play music, answer questions, and control smart home devices.

### 17.4.3 Healthcare

In the healthcare industry, AI agents can assist with diagnostics, patient monitoring, and personalized treatment plans. For example, AI agents are used to analyze medical images, predict disease progression, and recommend treatment options.

### 17.4.4 E-commerce

E-commerce platforms use AI agents to improve the customer experience by offering personalized recommendations, assisting with order tracking, and providing real-time customer support.

### 17.4.5 Financial Services

AI agents are employed in the financial sector to automate

trading, manage portfolios, and provide customer service through chatbots. These agents can make real-time decisions based on market conditions and user inputs.

## 17.5 Challenges in Building AI Agents

While AI agents have the potential to revolutionize industries, building effective agents comes with its own set of challenges:

### 17.5.1 Data Requirements

AI agents, particularly those based on machine learning, require large datasets for training. Obtaining and processing these datasets can be expensive and time-consuming.

### 17.5.2 Handling Uncertainty

Many environments in which AI agents operate are unpredictable, which can make it difficult for agents to perform reliably. Learning agents must be capable of adapting to unforeseen circumstances.

### 17.5.3 Ethical Considerations

**AI agents**, especially those that interact with humans, must be designed with ethical considerations in mind. This includes ensuring fairness, transparency, and data privacy in the agent's decision-making process.

### 17.5.4 Computational Resources

Training and deploying AI agents, particularly in complex environments, can be resource-intensive. High-performance hardware and cloud computing platforms are often required to handle the processing demands.

## 17.6 Conclusion

AI agents represent a transformative step in the evolution of AI, offering autonomous solutions that can operate independently in real-world environments. Whether it's managing customer service, controlling self-driving cars, or providing personalized healthcare, AI agents are poised to solve some of the most complex challenges across various industries. By learning how to build, train, and deploy AI agents, developers and organizations can leverage the power of autonomy to create innovative and impactful applications.

In the next chapter, we will dive deeper into the world of **Fine-Tuning LLMs**, where we explore how to optimize large language models for specific use cases.

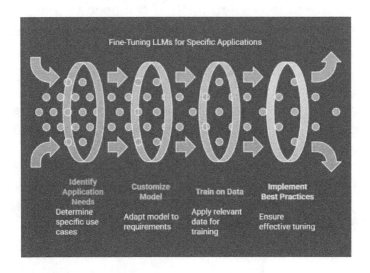

## 18.2 Why Fine-Tune LLMs?

**Fine-tuning pre-trained models** comes with several advantages:

**Cost Efficiency:** Training a new model from scratch can be expensive and time-consuming. Fine-tuning allows you to build on existing models with fewer resources.

**Task-Specific Expertise:** Pre-trained models are generally designed for general-purpose tasks. Fine-tuning enables them to specialize in areas like medical diagnosis, legal advice, or technical writing.

**Improved Accuracy:** By training the model on your domain-specific data, the model's accuracy and relevance in that domain increase, leading to better results for your intended use case.

**Adaptation to Business Needs:** Fine-tuning allows

organizations to tailor LLMs to their specific workflows, customer interactions, or industry language, making them more useful for real-world applications.

**Example:** A healthcare company fine-tuning an LLM on medical records and terminology to create an AI assistant capable of helping doctors with patient diagnosis.

## 18.3 The Fine-Tuning Process

Fine-tuning an LLM involves several steps, from selecting the right model to training it on specific datasets. Here's a breakdown of the process:

### 18.3.1 Selecting the Pre-Trained Model

The first step in fine-tuning is selecting a pre-trained model that aligns with your application needs. Models like **GPT-4, BERT**, and **T5** are commonly used for various NLP tasks such as text generation, summarization, and question-answering.

**GPT-4:** Ideal for creative tasks such as text generation, dialogue systems, and summarization.

**BERT:** Primarily used for sentence classification, translation, and question-answering tasks.

**T5:** Highly flexible for translation, summarization, and other **NLP** tasks that require complex transformations.

**Example:** If you're building a customer service bot, GPT-4 may be a suitable choice for its conversational abilities, while BERT might be better for document classification.

### 18.3.2 Preparing the Dataset

The dataset is a crucial component for fine-tuning. It should contain domain-specific examples relevant to the tasks the model will perform after fine-tuning. Data can be sourced from existing databases, customer records, or industry-specific content like technical documents or medical records.

**Data Labeling:** If you're fine-tuning a model for text classification or question-answering, ensure your dataset is properly labeled for the task.

**Data Cleaning:** Remove any inconsistencies, duplicate entries, or irrelevant information to improve the quality of the dataset.

**Example:** For a medical chatbot, your dataset should include patient conversations, common medical queries, and diagnostic notes, all properly anonymized and organized.

### 18.3.3 Fine-Tuning the Model

Once your dataset is ready, you can begin the fine-tuning process using available frameworks and tools such as Hugging Face, OpenAI, or PyTorch. Fine-tuning involves adjusting the weights of the pre-trained model based on the new dataset, allowing it to adapt to your specific requirements.

**Training Configuration:** During fine-tuning, set the hyperparameters such as learning rate, batch size, and training epochs, which control the speed and depth of training.

**Optimization:** Use optimization techniques like AdamW to adjust the model's weights and biases in a way that minimizes error and improves performance on your dataset.

**Example:** Fine-tuning GPT-4 on customer service dialogues by training it to handle various customer queries and issues, fine-tuning it over several epochs until it performs effectively in your specific domain.

### 18.3.4 Evaluating the Fine-Tuned Model

After fine-tuning, the model must be evaluated to ensure that it meets performance expectations. This involves using a validation dataset that the model hasn't seen during training to measure accuracy, precision, recall, and other performance metrics. If the model doesn't perform well, adjustments can be made to the dataset or training process.

**Metrics:** Evaluate your fine-tuned model using standard performance metrics like accuracy, F1 score, or BLEU score, depending on the task.

**Tuning and Retraining:** If the model underperforms, consider further fine-tuning, or retraining with additional data or altered hyperparameters.

**Example:** After fine-tuning a legal document summarizer, use a set of unseen legal documents to test the model's ability to provide accurate and concise summaries.

### 18.4 Tools for Fine-Tuning

Several tools and platforms make the process of fine-tuning LLMs accessible, even to developers without extensive machine learning expertise.

### 18.4.1 Hugging Face

Hugging Face is a popular open-source platform that provides pre-trained models, datasets, and tools for fine-tuning. Their model hub includes hundreds of models for various NLP tasks, and their Trainer API simplifies the fine-tuning process.

Transformers Library: Provides easy access to LLMs like **GPT, BERT, and T5.**

**Datasets Library:** Offers a wide range of pre-processed datasets to fine-tune your models.

**Training APIs:** Simplifies training by handling many low-level tasks like data loading, optimization, and evaluation.

### 18.4.2 OpenAI API

OpenAI provides a cloud-based API that allows developers to fine-tune models like GPT-4 without needing high-end hardware or extensive machine learning experience. OpenAI handles the underlying infrastructure, allowing developers to focus on providing the right datasets and monitoring performance.

**Fine-Tuning Interface:** A web-based interface that lets you upload data and configure your model for fine-tuning.

**Scalable Infrastructure:** Fine-tuning is done on OpenAI's cloud infrastructure, so you don't need to manage hardware resources.

### 18.4.3 PyTorch and TensorFlow

These deep learning libraries provide lower-level control for fine-tuning models. While they require more expertise compared to Hugging Face or OpenAI, they allow more customization and optimization for specific needs.

- **PyTorch:** Known for its flexibility and ease of use in research settings, PyTorch is ideal for experimenting with fine-tuning models.

- **TensorFlow:** Often used in production environments due to its scalability, TensorFlow is well-suited for large-scale fine-tuning projects.

### 18.5 Use Cases for Fine-Tuned LLMs

Fine-tuning LLMs can benefit a wide range of applications. Here are some common use cases:

### 18.5.1 Customer Service Automation

Fine-tuned models can automate customer service, responding to frequently asked questions, handling queries, and providing support. Fine-tuning makes these models better at understanding the specific needs of customers in various industries.

**Example:** A retail company fine-tunes GPT-4 to answer customer inquiries about product availability, return policies, and shipping.

### 18.5.2 Industry-Specific Content Generation

Businesses in industries like law, healthcare, and education often require specialized content generation. By fine-tuning LLMs, companies can create models that understand industry jargon and produce more relevant outputs.

**Example:** A law firm fine-tunes BERT to summarize legal contracts and suggest relevant clauses based on case history.

### 18.5.3 Personal Assistants

Fine-tuning can be used to create more personalized AI assistants that cater to specific user preferences, from managing calendars to offering tailored recommendations.

**Example:** Fine-tuning an LLM to serve as a personalized health advisor that can monitor a user's health metrics and offer advice based on medical records.

## 18.6 Best Practices for Fine-Tuning LLMs

Fine-tuning requires careful planning and execution to ensure optimal performance. Here are some best practices:

- **Quality Data:** Ensure that your dataset is high-quality, balanced, and representative of the tasks the model will be performing.

- **Data Privacy:** When working with sensitive data, such as customer or medical information, make sure that it is properly anonymized and complies with data protection regulations.

- **Avoid Overfitting:** Monitor the model for signs of overfitting, where it performs well on the training data but poorly on new data. This can be mitigated by using techniques like early stopping or regularization.

- **Hyperparameter Tuning:** Experiment with different hyperparameters to optimize your fine-tuned model's performance. Adjusting the learning rate or batch size can significantly impact results.

## 18.7 Conclusion

**Fine-tuning LLMs** offers a powerful way to create AI models that are specifically adapted to your needs without the cost of building models from scratch. With the right tools and practices, fine-tuning enables you to unlock the full potential of pre-trained models, whether you're looking to automate customer service, generate industry-specific content, or build personalized AI assistants. By mastering fine-tuning, you can harness the capabilities of AI to solve specialized problems in a wide variety of industries.

Thank you for embarking on this journey through the world of generative AI. By now, you've explored the incredible capabilities of Large Language Models (LLMs), from text generation to image creation, and learned how to apply these cutting-edge technologies to real-world applications. You've gained insights into building and fine-tuning AI models, responsibly integrating them into systems, and optimizing them for security, scalability, and ethical standards.

As AI continues to evolve at a rapid pace, the skills and knowledge you've gained from this ebook will position you at the forefront of innovation. Whether you're building AI-powered tools for your business, experimenting with creative applications, or simply deepening your understanding of AI, you now have the foundational tools to push the boundaries of what's possible.

The future of AI is bright, and the only limit is your imagination. Stay curious, keep experimenting, and continue exploring the vast potential that AI has to offer. This is just the beginning of your AI journey, and I hope this e-book has inspired you to dive deeper into this fascinating and ever-evolving field.

Once again, thank you for reading, and may your future endeavors in AI bring you both success and fulfillment.

Best regards,

**ANCHAL RANI**

Author and AI Enthusiast

ANCHAL RANI

# APPENDIX

This section provides detailed explanations of abbreviations and technical terms used in the e-book to enhance understanding and connect readers with the concepts.

- **AI (Artificial Intelligence):** AI refers to the simulation of human intelligence by machines. It encompasses learnin reasoning, and decision-making, enabling computers to perform tasks typically requiring human intelligence.

- **LLM (Large Language Model):** LLMs are machine learning models trained on vast text datasets to understand and generate human-like text. They are foundational to modern generative AI applications, such as **GPT** and **BERT**.

- **GPT (Generative Pre-trained Transformer):** GPT is an advanced LLM developed by OpenAI that excels in generating coherent and context-aware text. It is widely used for tasks like conversation, summarization, and creative writing.

- **API (Application Programming Interface):** APIs are sets of protocols and tools that allow different software applications to communicate with each other, enabling seamless integration and functionality.

- **UX (User Experience):** UX focuses on the overall experience of a user while interacting with a digital product. It aims to make applications intuitive, efficient, and enjoyable to you.

- **RAG (Retrieval Augmented Generation):** This framework combines traditional information retrieval techniques with generative AI to deliver accurate, contextually relevant responses in applications like search and knowledge systems.

- **NLP (Natural Language Processing):** A branch of AI dedicated to the interaction between computers and human languages, NLP enables systems to process, understand, and generate text or speech.

- **BERT (Bidirectional Encoder Representations from Transformers):** Developed by Google, BERT is a pre-trained NLP model that understands the context of words in a sentence by analyzing surrounding text.

- **FAISS (Facebook AI Similarity Search):** Faiss is a library created by Facebook for efficient similarity search clustering of dense vectors. It is often used in AI-powered search applications.

- **AWS (Amazon Web Services):** AWS is a cloud computing platform offering a range of services, including AI and ML tools, enabling scalable application development and deployment.

- **CSV (Comma-Separated Values):** A simple file format for storing tabular data in plain text, where values are separat by commas. It is commonly used for data storage and exchange.

- **UI (User Interface):** UI refers to the visual and interactive elements of an application that enable users to interact with the system, such as buttons, menus, and forms.

- **SDK (Software Development Kit):** SDKs are collections of software tools and libraries designed to help developers create applications for specific platforms or technologie ML (Machine Learning): A subset of AI that focuses on enabling systems to learn and improve from data without explicit programming.

- **OpenAI:** OpenAI is a leading research organization in AI, known for its work on GPT models and its commitment to developing safe and ethical AI technologies.

- **Hugging Face:** A popular platform and library for NLP and

ML that provides pre-trained models, datasets, and tools for building AI applications, widely adopted by developers and researchers.

- **TensorFlow:** An open-source ML framework developed by Google. It is widely used for building, training, and deploying AI models at scale.

- **PyTorch:** An open-source ML library created by Facebook. PyTorch is renowned for its ease of use and flexibility deep learning applications.

- **TF-IDF (Term Frequency-Inverse Document Frequency):** A statistical method used in text analysis to measure the importance of a word in a document relative to a collection of documents.

- **Embedding:** A technique for representing data (like text or images) as dense numerical vectors. Embeddings capture semantic meaning, enabling AI models to process the data effectively.

- **GAN (Generative Adversarial Network):** GANs are AI models consisting of two neural networks a generator and a discriminator that work together to create realistic synthetic data, such as images or videos.

- **Stable Diffusion:** An open-source model for generating high-quality images from text prompts. It is widely used for artistic and commercial purposes.

*This expanded appendix serves as a valuable resource, helping readers navigate the technical terms and concepts discussed throughout the ebook .*

## Final Review Of This Book

As we conclude ***The Power of Artificial Intelligence***, we hope this book has provided valuable insights into the evolving landscape of AI, large language models, and generative AI applications. From understanding foundational concepts to exploring real-world applications, our goal has been to make AI accessible, informative, and engaging for enthusiasts and professionals alike.

**Key Takeaways**

**The transformative impact of AI on industries and daily life
How LLMs and generative AI are shaping the
future of work, creativity, and automation
Ethical considerations and challenges in
decentralized AI development
The roadmap for AI's next decade—
opportunities and innovations**

**A Note of Gratitude**

This book is the result of extensive research, discussions, and a passion for making AI knowledge widely available. I sincerely thank all the experts, contributors, and early readers who provided invaluable feedback throughout this journey.

**What's Next?**

Artificial intelligence is evolving rapidly, and so is our understanding of its capabilities. Stay connected for updates, future editions, and discussions on the latest breakthroughs in AI.

**Join the Conversation!**

**- Share your thoughts and reviews online—your
feedback helps improve future editions.**

- Connect on AMAZON.COM for AI insights and discussions.
- Explore more AI resources and recommended readings at AMAZON.

If you found this book valuable, please leave a review on Amazon or your favorite platform—it helps others discover and benefit from it!

Thank you for being a part of this journey into the world of AI. The future is intelligent—let's shape it together!

www.ingramcontent.com/pod-product-compliance
Lightning Source LLC
LaVergne TN
LVHW022348060326
832902LV00022B/4306